HELEN PE ___ D.

QUICK GUIDE TO

Vitamins, Minerals and Supplements

SILOAM PRESS

QUICK GUIDE TO VITAMINS, MINERALS AND SUPPLEMENTS
by Helen Pensanti, M.D.
Published by Siloam Press
A part of Strang Communications Company
600 Rinehart Road
Lake Mary, Florida 32746
www.charismahouse.com

Unless otherwise noted, all Scripture quotations are from the King James
Version of the Bible.

Cover design by Judith McKittrick
Interior design by Pat Theriault

Library of Congress Catalog Card Number: 2002107792
International Standard Book Number: 0-88419-887-1

This book is not intended to provide medical advice or to take the place of
medical advice and treatment from your personal physician. Readers are
advised to consult their own doctors or other qualified health professionals
regarding the treatment of their medical problems. Neither the publisher nor
the author takes any responsibility for any possible consequences from any
treatment, action or application of medicine, supplement, herb or preparation
to any person reading or following the information in this book. If readers are
taking prescription medications, they should consult with their physicians
and not take themselves off of medicines to start supplementation without
the proper supervision of a physician.

02 03 04 05 06   87654321
Printed in the United States of America

Dedication

The idea for this book came from Paul and Jan Crouch, whose sincere concern for their viewers extends not only to their spiritual well-being but also to their physical well-being. Their valuable leadership to the body of Christ is unparalleled.

Thank you, Paul and Jan, for the many opportunities you have given me to minister to the TBN family in the years since 1985! This ministry opportunity has been one of my greatest pleasures.

Sweet Holy Spirit, I thank You for Your presence and wisdom, which has empowered me to walk the straight and narrow path to enjoy victory in Jesus.

From the Desk of Helen Pensanti, M.D.

A SPECIAL THANK YOU!

I want to thank Barbara Biski Hoffman, my dearest friend and the producer of my television program, *Doctor to Doctor,* for "riding shotgun" for me and for my ministry. The gifts and talents God has given me are being multiplied a hundredfold through Barbara's caring efforts as she tempers my weaknesses and sharpens and polishes my strengths.

Barbara has been intricately involved with this manuscript as well, making it possible for me to share effectively this message with you, the reader.

ACKNOWLEDGMENTS

I would also like to thank Kiana Groeters for typing the original draft of this manuscript at 150 words per minute. Whew! Now that's fast!

Many thanks to Andy Broadaway at OnlineMastery (www.onlinemastery.com), who spent hours helping to organize the material.

And special thanks to my dear viewers for their love, support and prayers. Your letters, e-mails and faxes over the years have been a source of encouragement to me as I often felt I was swimming against the tide when I tried to integrate natural treatments and mainstream medicine. Now, finally, we can see the progress as more and more studies are finalized that support the use of herbs and supplements. Thank you again for all of your support. My prayer for you always is for "better health—naturally!"

Cordially,
Helen Pensanti, M.D.

Table of Contents

Introduction

The unthinkable has happened—conventional medical doctors are recognizing the important role that vitamins, minerals, amino acids, natural herbal remedies and other supplements play in safeguarding our optimal health. The good news is that powerful studies have convinced many doctors that they can prevent, and even reverse, disease by recommending to their patients the proper use of natural supplements.

REASONS TO SUPPLEMENT

The following is a partial list of some of the more important reasons we need to add supplements to our diets:

- Nutrient-depleted soil
- Food additives (flavorings, preservatives, coloring, sweeteners, taste and aroma enhancers)
- Poorly balanced meals
- Environmental toxins and pollutants
- High sugar intake
- Aging bodies with different needs
- Stress
- Dieting
- Illness and disease

REVERSING DISEASE PROCESSES

A growing amount of scientific evidence is proving that natural supplements not only help us maintain optimal health and prevent disease; they actually help to reverse disease processes, including the dreaded "C" word—cancer. Many physicians have even conceded the wonderful antiaging properties that these natural nutrients provide.

With natural supplements so easily accessible, I feel strongly that all of us need to establish a good regimen for using them to insure optimal health for the rest of our lives. I have prepared this simple guide as a reference for you to help you establish a good, daily regimen.

RESPONSIBLE FOR MAINTENANCE

Our Creator wonderfully and intricately formed our bodies, and we are responsible to maintain them! It is a sad fact that we can no longer rely on our food to provide the nutrition we need due to increased depletion of our soil and overuse of chemicals in the production of crops. Part of the problem has been the disobedience of farmers to the divine agricultural laws established in God's Word as they relate to crop rotation and allowing the land to lie fallow so that it can be restored.

Along with the deteriorating quality of our foods, we also face the complicated problems of our society that threaten our health. Poor eating habits, increased stress and exposure to toxins result in a lessened ability of our bodies to absorb the nutrients we do ingest. These are strong reasons our bodies cry out for nutritional supplements.

RESPONDING TO YOUR QUESTIONS

While doctors and millions of people are accepting the fact that to insure health we must acknowledge our need for natural supplements, many of you are asking me the obvious questions:

- Dr. Helen, what supplements do I need?
- What is a good daily regimen for me?
- Does "one size fit all?"

This reference guide of vitamins, minerals, amino acids

and other supplements will help answer these questions as well as other questions posed to me. The special sections that apply to your health issues and your age-specific requirements will give you fingertip information to guide you.

And always remember: "A merry heart doeth good like a medicine" (Prov. 17:22).

Helen Pensanti, M.D.

Before You Read On

Because of the hype of big business surrounding nutritional supplements, it is essential for you to have a working definition of the basic terms as used in this guide for various nutrients.

DEFINITION OF TERMS

- **Vitamin:** A complex organic substance found variously in most foods, or sometimes synthesized in the body, and essential, in small amounts, for the regulation of the metabolism and normal growth and functioning of the body.[1]

- **Mineral:** Any element or inorganic compound needed by plants and animals for proper growth and functioning, as iron, phosphorus or nitrate.[2]

- **Amino acid:** Any of a large group of organic acids that link together into polypeptide chains to form proteins that are necessary for all life. Ten of these (essential amino acids) cannot be synthesized by the human body and must be consumed.[3]

- **Supplement:** A general term for something added, especially to make up for a lack or deficiency.[4] Relating to nutrition, the word *supplement* is a collective term for all vital nutrients that should be added to our nutritional regimen because of depletion of soil and degeneration of modern diets.

For our purposes, the Other Natural Supplements section of this book will include vital substances that do not fit into the specific categories of vitamins, minerals or amino acids.

RECOMMENDED DAILY ALLOWANCES

Some of the recommended doses for vitamins and minerals in this guide will be higher than the RDA (recommended daily allowance) normally seen.

The federal government first formulated RDA guidelines during World War II (1941–1945) to reduce diseases that were attributed to severe deficiencies, diseases such as scurvy and beriberi. Many researchers believe that in today's times of stress and illness, the RDAs formulated in 1941 are severely inadequate for the promotion of health.

OPTIMAL DAILY ALLOWANCE

Extensive scientific research has shown that nutrient levels that are far above the suggested RDA are most beneficial in preventing disease.

People who take only the suggested recommended daily allowances are still developing heart disease, cancer, diabetes, immune system disorders and viral infections because RDAs do not address the levels of nutrients necessary to attain optimal health. For that reason, health practitioners have coined the phrase *optimal daily allowance* (ODA), which refers to the dose believed to be necessary to achieve not just survival, but optimal health.

AVAILABLE SUPPLEMENT FORMS

Most supplements are available for consumption in several forms. You may have an individual preference for one form over the other based on your personal needs.

- **Tablets:** The most common form of supplement is easy to carry and store. Tablets have a very long shelf life. There is also little possibility that they can be adulterated in any way.

- **Caplets:** These are tablets shaped like a capsule. Usually they are coated so that they are protected from stomach acid and will dissolve in the intestine.
- **Capsules:** These are usually used for all oil-soluble vitamins like A, D and E.
- **Gel Capsules:** Soft capsules are easier to swallow than regular capsules.
- **Powders:** Powders are extra potent and are also good for people with allergies because they contain no fillers or additives.
- **Liquids:** This form of supplement is easy to swallow.

STORING SUPPLEMENTS

If you store your supplements in a cool, dark place and keep them well sealed, the shelf life should be two to three years for unopened jars or bottles and one year after they are opened. I do not advise that you refrigerate supplements because moisture can decrease the potency of some products.

THE BOTTOM LINE

This book is organized in a way to help you choose *easily* which vitamins, minerals and supplements you need to take.

If your goal is to restore your body to optimal health and keep it there, this book is for *YOU!*

Vitamins

Vitamins are organic substances that are derived from plants and animal products. With a few exceptions, they are not produced or manufactured by the body, but are needed daily for proper function of the body.

The word *vitamin* comes from a compound root—*vit-amine*. An *amine* is a nitrogen-containing chemical compound, and the prefix, *vit*, indicates it is vital to life. So a vitamin is an amine that is vital for life.

Vital functions that vitamins perform include:

- Supporting the normal functioning of our organs

- Helping the body utilize food

- Acting as catalysts for the body's biochemical processes, including blood formation, nerve transmission, protein metabolism and even hormone formation

A normal life is impossible without vitamins; we must get them either from our food or from nutritional supplements.

Vitamin A
(Beta Carotene Form)

NUTRIENT INFORMATION

- The carotene form is more commonly used and has shown no toxicity at high doses.
- Some of the beta carotene found in the form of fruits and vegetables is converted into vitamin A by your body. Carotene is, therefore, called pro-vitamin A.
- The animal source of vitamin A is called Retinol.
- Vitamin A is measured in USP (United States Pharmacopoeia) and IU (International Units). It may also be measured in RE (Retinol Equivalents).
- Vitamin A is stored in the body. (Note: Nutrients that are stored in the body are beneficial because the body can draw on its reserves when needed. However, you must be cautious not to consume consistently high amounts, which could create a toxic condition. In other words, take only recommended doses.)

BENEFITS FOR YOUR BODY

- Supports the immune system and protects the body from colds, flu and infections
- Known to be a factor in cancer prevention
- Helps reduce risk of heart disease
- Aids in treatment of emphysema, upper respiratory and lung disease
- Important for strong bones and healthy teeth and gums
- Helpful in reproductive processes and healthy sperm
- Aids in preventing night blindness and strengthening weak eyesight
- Helpful in the treatment of other eye disorders such as macular degeneration and retinitis pigmentosa

- Promotes healthy hair and skin
- Effective in the treatment of acne and the elimination of superficial wrinkles when applied topically

BEST NATURAL SOURCES
- Liver, fish oil, carrots, dark green vegetables, yellow vegetables, yellow fruit (apricots, cantaloupe), eggs

HOW TO SUPPLEMENT
- Recommended dose: 5,000–10,000 IU daily
- Not to exceed 40,000 IU daily

EXCESS/LACK
- Excess can cause liver enlargement.
- Deficiency causes night blindness.

TOXICITY ISSUES
- 50,000 IU daily for a long period is toxic to adults.
- 18,500 IU daily is toxic to infants.
- 30,000 IU daily can cause yellowing of skin.

DOCTOR'S COMMENTS
- Eat carrots! Carrots are extremely rich in beta carotene. Two large carrots will give you approximately 10,000 IU of vitamin A.
- Vitamin A should not be taken with the acne drug Accutane.
- Pregnant women should not take vitamin A, but can take beta carotene without adverse effects.

Vitamin B Complex

NUTRIENT INFORMATION

- The B "family" consists of B1 (thiamin); B2 (riboflavin); B3 (niacin); B5 (pantothenic acid); B6 (pyridoxine); B12 (cyanocobalamin); B15 (pangamic acid); biotin, choline, folic acid, inositol and PABA (para-aminobenzoic acid). We will discuss each of these separately in the following pages (with the exception of B15, which is not a common supplement taken alone).
- Vitamin B complex is a supplement formulated to include several of the B vitamins. Even if you take other B vitamins separately, it is good to add a B complex supplement because these vitamins work best together and will make your regimen more effective.
- They are water soluble, so daily consumption is required.
- B complex often turns the urine bright yellow. This is from vitamin B2, which is naturally yellow. Any excess that your body does not use is excreted.
- Stress, poor diet and alcohol rapidly deplete your body of B vitamins.

BENEFITS FOR YOUR BODY

- Produce energy, reducing fatigue
- Diminish anxiety
- Treat depression
- Note: See individual members of B family discussed for comprehensive benefits of B vitamins.

Vitamin B1
(Thiamin)

NUTRIENT INFORMATION

- This important vitamin is water soluble, which makes daily consumption necessary.
- Eating large quantities of fast food frequently can lead to a deficiency of B1.
- B1 is an antioxidant. (Note: Antioxidants protect cells from the damaging effects of oxygen free radicals that occur during normal cell metabolism.[1])

BENEFITS FOR YOUR BODY

- Plays a major role in energy production
- Supports the brain and nervous system
- Improves circulation
- Required for production of red blood cells
- May help reduce diabetic neuropathy (numbness and tingling in extremities)
- May help with symptoms of herpes zoster
- Supports immune system
- Supports adrenal glands
- Improves digestion
- Necessary for carbohydrate metabolism

BEST NATURAL SOURCES

- Brewer's yeast, beans and peas, wheat germ, oatmeal, peanuts

HOW TO SUPPLEMENT

- Recommended dose: 25–100 mg. daily
- Works best if taken with a B complex supplement

EXCESS/LACK

- A deficiency of thiamine can cause fatigue, "foggy brain" syndrome, heart palpitations and problems with vision.
- Other symptoms include diarrhea, weight loss, pins and needles in fingers and toes, muscle weakness and dizziness. Deficiencies of B1 are often found in psychiatric patients and alcoholics.
- Deficiency of B1 also causes beriberi.

TOXICITY ISSUES

- Rare—not stored in the body

DOCTOR'S COMMENTS

- I always include B1 in my PMS formula because of its mild diuretic properties and its positive effect on the nervous system and mental attitude. I like to use it in conjunction with B2, B6, B12 and magnesium.

Vitamin B2
(Riboflavin)

NUTRIENT INFORMATION
- Riboflavin is water soluble, so daily consumption is required.
- It gives urine its yellow color after consumption of multi-B vitamins.
- B2 can also act as an antioxidant.

BENEFITS FOR YOUR BODY
- Helps turn food into energy
- Assists in the formation of red blood cells
- Helps body produce antibodies for immune function
- Very important in reproduction and pregnancy

BEST NATURAL SOURCES
- Brewer's yeast, spinach, asparagus, eggs, yogurt, beans, fish, organ meats, spinach

HOW TO SUPPLEMENT
- Recommended dose is 25–100 mg. daily
- Best if taken with a B complex supplement

EXCESS/LACK
- A deficiency can lead to sore mouth (cracks at corners) and sore tongue, light sensitivity and watery or blood-shot eyes.

TOXICITY ISSUES
- None known

DOCTOR'S COMMENTS
- If you are pregnant or trying to get pregnant, be sure to get at least 50 mg. B2 in your multiple vitamin. A lack of B2 can damage a developing fetus.

Vitamin B3
(Niacin)

 NUTRIENT INFORMATION

- Niacin is water soluble, so daily consumption is required.
- It has a reputation as a health-heart vitamin.
- It is necessary for healthy functioning of the brain and nerves.
- Deficiencies of B3 are often found in elderly people with dementia and confusion.

 BENEFITS FOR YOUR BODY

- Reduces cholesterol and triglyceride levels
- Can raise HDL (good) cholesterol levels
- Aids metabolism
- Improves blood flow
- Assists in production of sex hormones
- Reduces sweet cravings
- Helps keep skin healthy, fights acne
- Helps relieve headaches, including migraines
- Enhances memory
- Reduces dizziness of Meniere's disease
- Treats headaches and other symptoms of alcohol consumption

 BEST NATURAL SOURCES

- Fish, lean meat, poultry, brewer's yeast, wheat germ, eggs, nuts, legumes.

HOW TO SUPPLEMENT

- Usual dose is 100–400 mg. daily
- To lower cholesterol, you need the inositol hexaniacinate form. Higher doses may be required and subsequently lowered as cholesterol goes down. Check with your physician.

EXCESS/LACK

- A deficiency of niacin can cause bad breath and severe skin rashes.
- Deficiency disease is called pellagra. The symptoms are dementia, diarrhea and an inflamed tongue. It is very rare in the U.S.

TOXICITY ISSUES

- Toxicity is rare.
- Extremely high continuous doses can lead to liver damage.

DOCTOR'S COMMENTS

- If you are taking a separate supplement of niacin in addition to your B complex, avoid taking it on an empty stomach to avoid gastrointestinal distress.
- Do not supplement with plain niacin if you have gout or ulcers. Choose inositol hexanicotinate, instead.
- CAUTION: Some forms of niacin can cause flushing of the skin, stomach irritation and itching. Two forms of niacin, inositol hexaniacinate and niacinamide, do not cause these side effects.[2]

Vitamin B5
(Pantothenic Acid)

 NUTRIENT INFORMATION

- Pantothenic acid is water soluble, so daily consumption is required.
- It is known as the antistress vitamin, providing wonderful support for exhausted adrenal glands.
- Vitamin B5 aids the adrenal glands in manufacturing hormones.
- It is vital for tissue health.

 BENEFITS FOR YOUR BODY

- Helps fight stress and fatigue
- Helps relieve allergies and asthma
- Helps relieve arthritis
- Helps relieve headaches
- Helps treat and prevent depression and anxiety
- Helps prevent anemia
- Helps relieve psoriasis
- Aids in wound healing and fighting infections

 BEST NATURAL SOURCES

- Wheat germ, whole grains, blackstrap molasses, brewer's yeast, nuts, eggs

 HOW TO SUPPLEMENT

- Usual dose is 200–1,000 mg. daily, depending on stress level.

 EXCESS/LACK

- Lack of B5 may lead to depression, frequent infections and tingling in hands and feet.

TOXICITY ISSUES
- None known

 **DOCTOR'S COMMENTS**
- If you are undergoing a period of stress, are anemic or are suffering from extreme fatigue, I strongly suggest you supplement with vitamin B5 along with a good B complex.

Vitamin B6
(Pyridoxine)

 NUTRIENT INFORMATION

- B6 is actually a group of substances—pyridoxine, pyridoxal and pyridoxamine—that function together.
- Vitamin B6 is water soluble, so daily consumption is required.
- It is vital to adrenal gland health and function.
- B6 is known for having a positive effect on water retention and PMS symptoms.
- Food dyes, birth control pills and high-protein diets can lead to B6 deficiency. Be careful!
- People with carpal tunnel syndrome are often deficient in B6.
- Pyridoxine is critical for red blood cell production.
- Deficiencies of vitamin B6 are often found in elderly people with dementia and confusion, as well as in diabetics.

 BENEFITS FOR YOUR BODY

- Decreases your risk of heart attack and heart disease by decreasing homocysteine levels when taken with folic acid
- Relieves acne
- Aids mental clarity and brain function
- Enhances immune system
- Balances hormone and water levels (mild diuretic)
- Helps relieve allergies and asthma
- Relieves carpal tunnel syndrome
- Helps relieve morning sickness
- Reduces peripheral neuropathy, especially in diabetics
- Treats or prevents anemia

BEST NATURAL SOURCES

- Wheat, soy beans, black strap molasses, spinach, cantaloupe, eggs, peanuts, fish

HOW TO SUPPLEMENT

- Usual dose: 100 mg. daily
- Best if taken with a B complex supplement to prevent an imbalance
- Also available in time-release capsules

EXCESS/LACK

- Lack of B6 can lead to anemia and neuropathy (tingling in fingers and toes).
- Lack of B6 can also lead to depression.

TOXICITY ISSUES

- Do not take more than 300 mg. daily to avoid neurological or liver damage.

DOCTOR'S COMMENTS

- Everyone should be taking B6 and folic acid daily to reduce their risk of heart attack.
- I recommend 150 mg. per day for PMS patients.
- My favorite form of vitamin B6 is a time-release capsule.

Vitamin B12
(Cyanocobalamin)

NUTRIENT INFORMATION

- Vitamin B12 is water soluble; therefore, daily consumption is necessary.
- It is known as the "red" vitamin.
- Alcohol destroys vitamin B12.
- It is often deficient in the elderly.

BENEFITS FOR YOUR BODY

- Assists in formation of red blood cells, helping to prevent anemia
- Helps reduce risk of heart attacks by lowering homocysteine levels
- Diminishes fatigue and helps increase energy levels
- Helps relieve allergies
- Improves concentration and ability to learn and remember
- Helps protect against smoking-induced cancers
- Helpful to multiple sclerosis patients because it helps form and maintain the myelin sheath, which covers the nerves
- Helps prevent graying of hair and balding

BEST NATURAL SOURCES

- Liver, beef, fish, eggs, cheese, poultry

HOW TO SUPPLEMENT

- Usual dose is 100–400 mcg. daily.

EXCESS/LACK
- A deficiency of B12 can lead to pernicious anemia, depression and fatigue.
- Vitamin B12 deficiency is often found in Alzheimer's patients.

TOXICITY ISSUES
- None known

DOCTOR'S COMMENTS
- If you are a vegetarian and do not eat eggs, cheese or milk, then you need B12 supplementation.
- The body quickly absorbs the sublingual form of B12 better than a capsule that must pass through the stomach and digestive system.
- If there is a severe vitamin B12 deficiency, leading to extreme fatigue or severe loss of cognitive function in the elderly, I recommend a weekly B12 injection until the condition is resolved.

Biotin

NUTRIENT INFORMATION
- Biotin is another member of the B complex family and is also water soluble.
- It is used by the body to metabolize carbohydrates, fat and protein.
- Biotin is needed by the body for the development of white blood cells.
- Diabetics often have low biotin levels.

BENEFITS FOR YOUR BODY
- Prevents baldness and helps keep hair from turning gray
- Enhances utilization of insulin (good for diabetes)
- Helps treat psoriasis, eczema, dermatitis and dandruff
- Helps keep skin healthy
- Keeps immune system strong

BEST NATURAL SOURCES
- Egg yolk, brewer's yeast, nuts, molasses, soybeans

HOW TO SUPPLEMENT
- Usual dose is 50–200 mcg.
- It works best in combination with the other B vitamins and is usually found in B complex.

EXCESS/LACK
- Lack of biotin can cause hair to turn gray; also, a deficiency can lead to severe exhaustion and depression.

TOXICITY ISSUES
- None known

DOCTOR'S COMMENTS

- If you are tired and pale and have a sore tongue, you may be deficient in biotin.
- Also, anyone who eats raw egg whites is subject to biotin deficiency because a chemical in the egg white causes the body to excrete biotin. I do not recommend eating raw eggs, but if you do, take note.
- Anecdotal evidence exists that 100 mg. of biotin daily may prevent hair loss in some men.

Choline

NUTRIENT INFORMATION

- Choline is a member of the B family.
- It is one of the few substances that can penetrate the blood brain barrier.
- Acetylcholine, an important brain nutrient, cannot be produced in the body without choline.
- Cooking often destroys the choline in foods.
- Without choline, cell membranes would degenerate.
- It aids in gallbadder and liver function.

BENEFITS FOR YOUR BODY

- Promotes brain health
- Prevents build up of fat in the liver; helps detox the liver
- Helps diminish/treat ringing in ears
- May help retard aging of the brain (helps keep synapses healthy)
- May help reduce and prevent asthma attacks
- May aid in treatment of Alzheimer's disease
- Helps combat anxiety and stress by "calming the brain"
- May be beneficial for Parkinson's disease

BEST NATURAL SOURCES

- Egg yolks, soybeans, lecithin, meat, legumes, cabbage

HOW TO SUPPLEMENT

- Usual dose is 200–500 mg. daily.

EXCESS/LACK

- A deficiency of choline may lead to cirrhosis of the liver.

TOXICITY ISSUES

- None known

DOCTOR'S COMMENTS

- If you are having problems with memory, I strongly suggest adding choline to your vitamin regimen.
- People who drink alcohol should be aware of getting enough choline to help support their liver.
- Choline and inositol may help thinning hair and baldness.

Folic Acid
(Folate)

NUTRIENT INFORMATION

- Folic acid is one of the most common vitamin deficiencies.
- It is water soluble, so daily consumption is necessary.
- It is essential for the formation of red blood cells.
- A deficiency of folic acid can lead to anemia.
- Many people with dementia and mental confusion are found to be deficient in folic acid.
- Low folic acid and elevated homocysteine levels have been associated with Alzheimer's disease.
- It is necessary for proper cell division, so it is extremely important in early pregnancy to have normal levels.

BENEFITS FOR YOUR BODY

- Protects against birth defects of spina bifida and other neural tube defects
- Helps lower homocysteine levels to reduce risk of heart disease and heart attack
- Prevents canker sores
- Relieves symptoms of gout
- Helps treat acne
- Helps prevent gingivitis and periodontal disease
- Helps reduce restless leg syndrome
- May help in treating cervical dysplasia and cervical cancer according to some studies
- Enhances immune system
- Aids in treatment of depression
- Helps provide nourishment for the brain to prevent dementia

- May help low sex drive or impotence
- May help restore gray hair to its natural color

BEST NATURAL SOURCES

- Dark green leafy vegetables (like spinach and kale), asparagus, soy beans, peas, egg yolk, cantaloupe, apricots

HOW TO SUPPLEMENT

- Usually supplied in 400 mcg. and 800 mcg. strengths
- Recommended dose: 800 mcg. daily

EXCESS/LACK

- Deficiency may lead to anemia, headaches and heart palpitations.
- Large doses of folic acid may interfere with some cancer drugs.
- High doses of folic acid should not be used by anyone with a seizure disorder.

TOXICITY ISSUES

- Rare

DOCTOR'S COMMENTS

- I strongly recommend a supplement regimen that includes folic acid and vitamin B6 since the data is so overwhelming that this can dramatically lower your risk of heart attack.
- For women of childbearing age, studies have shown that a daily intake of 400 mcg. can prevent most neural tube defects. This regimen must begin prior to conception as the first six weeks of a fetus's development are the most critical. (This is before many women even know they are pregnant.)
- All elderly people and all women on birth control should take folic acid.
- Check your multiple vitamins to make sure you are getting at least 400 mcg. daily.

Inositol

NUTRIENT INFORMATION
- Inositol is a member of the B family.
- Multiple sclerosis patients are often deficient in inositol.
- It is vital for hair growth.

BENEFITS FOR YOUR BODY
- It supports eye health.
- It helps lower cholesterol.
- It helps prevent hardening of the arteries.
- It helps with diabetic neuropathy.
- It enhances REM sleep (dream sleep).
- It helps detox the liver.
- High doses have been used to treat depression and obsessive-compulsive behavior.
- In conjunction with choline, inositol may help diminish PMS symptoms.

BEST NATURAL SOURCES
- Whole grains, organ meats, legumes, raisins, lecithin

HOW TO SUPPLEMENT
- Inositol is usually found in B complex supplements in doses of 25–250 mg.
- 100 mg. would be a good dose.

EXCESS/LACK
- Lack believed to contribute to symptoms of hair loss

TOXICITY ISSUES
- None known

DOCTOR'S COMMENTS

- Anyone who consumes alcohol or high levels of caffeine may have a shortage of inositol and require supplementation.
- Inositol and choline may help prevent thinning hair and baldness.

PABA

(Para-aminobenzoic Acid)

NUTRIENT INFORMATION

- PABA is a member of the B family.
- It aids in the metabolism of amino acids.
- It helps support growth of healthy intestinal flora.
- It supports the body's production of B12.

BENEFITS FOR YOUR BODY

- Protects skin from negative effects of UV light (sunburn, cancer)
- Promotes healthy skin
- May delay graying of hair when used in conjunction with pantothenic acid (B5)
- Helps relieve anxiety

BEST NATURAL SOURCES

- Brewer's yeast, cantaloupe, raisins, eggs

HOW TO SUPPLEMENT

- Usually found in B complex supplements in doses of 50–100 mg.
- Also available separately in regular and time-release capsules

EXCESS/LACK

- Deficiency may lead to eczema.
- PABA may interfere with some cancer-fighting drugs.

TOXICITY ISSUES

- Toxicity is rare.
- Extremely high continuous doses are not advised because they could cause liver damage.

DOCTOR'S COMMENTS

- PABA is often used to protect against sunburn and also may protect against wrinkling of the skin at the same time.
- Note: Some people are allergic to PABA.

Bioflavonoids

(Citrus Bioflavonoids, Rutin, Hesperidin and Quercetin)

NUTRIENT INFORMATION

- Bioflavonoids are plant pigments.
- They cannot be produced by the body, so they must be supplied by the diet.
- They are called vitamin P (for permeability) because they increase capillary strength.
- Flavonoids are the substances that provide the yellow and orange color in citrus fruits.
- They are often found in vitamin C supplement complexes as they promote proper absorption of vitamin C.
- Bioflavonoids have antioxidant properties.
- They strengthen cell membranes and make them more resistant to viruses and infections.
- Quercetin helps reduce inflammation and is an antiviral and antihistamine agent.

BENEFITS FOR YOUR BODY

- Strengthen the walls of capillaries
- May be an effective remedy for varicose veins, hemorrhoids and bruises
- Natural immune boosters that help build resistance to infection
- May be powerful anticancer agents, especially quercetin
- Help improve blood circulation throughout the body, including the skin
- Help maintain collagen and connective tissue
- Quercetin helpful in reducing allergy and asthma symptoms
- Helpful in respiratory tract infections

BEST NATURAL SOURCES

- The white material just below the peel of citrus fruits such as lemons, oranges and grapefruits; also found in buckwheat, blackberries and cherries
- Quercetin found in onions, grapes and zucchini

HOW TO SUPPLEMENT

- May be found in a C complex or sold separately
- Usually found in a ratio of 500 mg. of bioflavonoids to 50 mg. of rutin and hesperidin
- Most common dose: 500–2000 mg. daily

EXCESS/LACK

- Deficiency may manifest as deep red bruises on hands or arms and/or edema (accumulation of fluid in the bodily tissues).

TOXICITY ISSUES

- None known

DOCTOR'S COMMENTS

- Many menopausal patients have found effective relief from hot flashes with an increase in bioflavonoids.
- Use bioflavonoids if your gums bleed when you brush your teeth.
- A ten-year study showed that citrus bioflavonoids might help prevent miscarriage or premature labor.

Vitamin C

NUTRIENT INFORMATION

- Almost all animals synthesize their own vitamin C; however, humans do not.
- Vitamin C is a powerful antioxidant that protects the body from free-radical damage.
- It has antiviral properties.
- It increases the body's activity of white blood cells, antibodies and T cells, thus enhancing immune function.
- Vitamin C helps support adrenal glands, especially in times of stress.
- Healthy vitamin C levels are associated with increased life expectancy.
- Ascorbic acid is the synthetic form of vitamin C and may be irritating to sensitive stomachs.
- It is critically important in the formation of collagen, which is vital for cartilage and connective tissue and important for repair of wounds and healthy blood vessels.

BENEFITS FOR YOUR BODY

- Enhances immune system
- May help protect against many types of cancer
- Reduces risk of heart disease
- Helps prevent and fight bacterial infections
- Helps maintain healthy gum and mouth tissue
- Prevents blood clots and atherosclerosis
- Reduces the duration and symptoms of the common cold
- Reduces frequency and severity of asthma attacks (many asthmatics found to be deficient in vitamin C)
- May help halt formation of cataracts by minimizing damage caused by ultraviolet light

- Accelerates wound and post-op healing by aiding the production of collagen
- Helpful for anemia because it enhances the absorption of iron
- Helps elevate HDL (good) cholesterol
- High doses may help reduce symptoms of allergies, including food allergies.
- May improve tolerance to glucose in Type II diabetes

BEST NATURAL SOURCES

- Citrus fruits, broccoli, cantaloupe, peppers, kiwi fruit, strawberries, green leafy vegetables

HOW TO SUPPLEMENT

- Usual dose is 500–1,000 mg. three times daily.
- It is best to take vitamin C in divided doses to increase absorption. Try 500 mg. four times per day to see if you can tolerate it without loose stools. If not, lower dose slightly to find your best daily dose.
- At first symptoms of a cold, take 2,000–6,000 mg. daily. This can cut the length and severity of the cold by about 30 percent.
- The best form of vitamin C contains bioflavonoids, hesperidan and rutin from rose hips.

EXCESS/LACK

- An excess of vitamin C can cause loose bowels or diarrhea.
- A lack of vitamin C leads to bleeding gums, bruising and frequent viral infections.
- Scurvy is a severe deficiency of vitamin C resulting in soft, bleeding gums, extreme weakness and hemorrhages under the skin. It is extremely rare in the Western world.

TOXICITY ISSUES

- Rare

DOCTOR'S COMMENTS

- Increase your intake of vitamin C during times of stress and exposure to environmental pollutants. Stress increases our excretion of this important vitamin.

- Inform your doctor if you are taking large doses of vitamin C as it may alter the results of some blood or urine tests.

- Large amounts of vitamin C may also interfere with the blood-thinning properties of Coumadin.

- High doses are not recommended for people with genetic conditions that cause iron overload (like thalassemia) because vitamin C enhances the absorption of iron.

- If you're taking high doses of vitamin C, be sure to take a magnesium supplement to guard against kidney stone formation.

- Be careful of taking too much chewable vitamin C as this may lead to erosion of tooth enamel.

Vitamin D

NUTRIENT INFORMATION

- Vitamin D is known as the "sunshine vitamin" because the sun's ultraviolet rays act on the skin to produce vitamin D, which is then absorbed by the body.
- Exposure to sunlight for at least fifteen minutes daily aids the body in producing vitamin D.
- It is essential for maintenance of bone density. Without vitamin D, calcium cannot be utilized to build bones.
- Vitamin D is fat soluble; the body stores excess in fat tissues.
- Note: Some vitamins are oil soluble, while others are water soluble. Water-soluble vitamins must be taken into the body daily because they cannot be stored and are excreted within a few days. Oil-soluble vitamins can be stored in the body's fatty tissue and the liver. Their digestion is improved when taken with meals that contain fat.
- It is measured in International Units (IU) or micrograms (mcg.).

BENEFITS FOR YOUR BODY

- Helps the body utilize calcium and phosphorus necessary for strong bones and teeth
- Helps treat immune system disorders
- Helps prevent osteoporosis and calcium deficiency
- Helps in treatment of conjunctivitis and glaucoma
- Helps with proper thyroid function

BEST NATURAL SOURCES

- Fish liver oils, fortified dairy products, salmon, tuna, herring, sardines.
- Vegetables not a good source

HOW TO SUPPLEMENT

- It is usually supplied in 400 IU capsules.
- Take 400–800 IU daily.

EXCESS/LACK

- Too much vitamin D leads to excessive calcification of tissues and can cause impaired kidney or liver function, unusual thirst, sore eyes and itching skin.
- A deficiency of vitamin D causes rickets, a disease that causes weak, soft, bowed leg bones.
- Lack of vitamin D can also cause severe tooth decay and osteoporosis.

TOXICITY ISSUES

- Do not take over 3,000 IU per day to avoid toxicity.
- Dosages of over 1,800 IU daily may cause toxicity in children.

DOCTOR'S COMMENTS

- Night workers and housebound people who do not get sunlight need increased levels of vitamin D.
- Elderly people should be sure to increase intake of vitamin D because our ability to produce vitamin D in the skin declines and our ability to absorb it decreases as we age.
- Some dairy products are not good sources of vitamin D because the form of vitamin D added is the synthetic form of vitamin D2. Check the label.

Vitamin E

NUTRIENT INFORMATION

- Vitamin E is a fat-soluble vitamin, but it can be stored in the body for a limited period of time.
- It is measured in International Units (IU); 1 IU of Vitamin E is equivalent to 1 mg.
- Vitamin E may be one of the most powerful nutrients that exists in terms of effectiveness; it is able to neutralize free radicals and is a very potent and active antioxidant, protecting against damage to cell membranes.
- It helps protect the body against toxins from environment as well as the ill effects of alcohol, estrogen and smoke.
- Low levels of vitamin E are believed to be a strong indicator of a potential heart attack.

BENEFITS FOR YOUR BODY

- Lowers cholesterol
- Slows progression of Alzheimer's disease
- Prevents heart disease and heart attacks
- Reduces platelet aggregation and helps prevent atherosclerosis
- Research indicates protection against various forms of cancer, including skin, lung, breast, prostate and cervical
- Prevents and dissolves blood clots
- Promotes healthy hair and skin
- Helps treat fibrocystic breast disease
- Improves glucose utilization and insulin reaction
- Helps reduce hot flashes in premenopausal and menopausal women
- Improves brain health
- May normalize hormone levels in women with PMS
- Acts as a diuretic and helps lower blood pressure

- Aids in prevention of miscarriages
- Lowers risk of developing cataracts
- Helps reduce pain and inflammation in the body, especially muscle cramps and painful leg cramps
- Decreases risk of Alzheimer's disease
- Enhances immune system, especially in the elderly

BEST NATURAL SOURCES

- Oils (corn, sunflower, safflower, soy), wheat germ, whole wheat, nuts (especially almonds), spinach

HOW TO SUPPLEMENT

- Usual dose is 400–1,200 IU daily.
- Best form is d–alpha tocopherol, which is natural and best absorbed. DL–alpha tocopherol is a synthetic form.
- Products that combine selenium with vitamin E increase the effectiveness of the vitamin E.
- All women who are menopausal should take 800 IU of vitamin E daily to help prevent hot flashes and to protect the heart.
- Women with PMS should take 400–800 IU daily to relieve PMS symptoms, especially breast tenderness.

EXCESS/LACK

- Deficiency of vitamin E leaves the body susceptible to damage from environmental free radicals. Symptoms of deficiency include anemia, decreased fertility, eye problems and difficulty walking.

TOXICITY ISSUES

- Rare. Extremely high doses may cause nausea, double-vision, intestinal cramps and diarrhea.

DOCTOR'S COMMENTS

- Most people are unable to get adequate amounts of vitamin E from food and need supplementation.
- If you are taking anticoagulants or having surgery,

check with your physician before taking vitamin E because it can interfere with the absorption of vitamin K, which helps blood clotting.

- Vitamin E loses potency when it is exposed to air, light and heat, so store in a cool, dark place.
- Take vitamin E with meals containing oils to increase absorption.
- I do not recommend iron supplements, but if you are taking iron, be aware that it can destroy vitamin E. Take them at least eight hours apart.

Vitamin K

NUTRIENT INFORMATION
- Vitamin K is fat soluble; it is stored in fatty tissue.
- Vitamin K aids the production of prothrombin, which is necessary for proper blood clotting.
- The body is able to manufacture vitamin K from good bacteria found in the intestinal tract.

BENEFITS FOR YOUR BODY
- Promotes proper blood clotting
- Promotes healthy liver function
- Has been used to treat nausea during pregnancy
- Necessary for proper bone mineralization
- Helps reduce heavy menstrual flow
- Helps treat jaundice and cirrhosis of the liver

BEST NATURAL SOURCES
- Leafy green vegetables, broccoli, soybeans, liver, wheat bran, blackstrap molasses, tomatoes

- Also found in meat, milk, eggs, and fruits

HOW TO SUPPLEMENT
- Supplementation is not usually necessary as most people get enough vitamin K from diet.
- If necessary, usual dose is 30–100 mcg.

EXCESS/LACK
- Deficiency can cause blood clotting and abnormal bleeding (nose bleeds and gastrointestinal bleeding).

TOXICITY ISSUES
- Extremely large doses (over 500 mcg.) can be toxic.

DOCTOR'S COMMENTS
- If you are taking blood-thinning medications, consult your physician before adding vitamin K because it promotes the formation of blood clots.
- You may have heard of vitamin K cream. Some people say that it has helped them fade spider veins and heal bruises. Most of these reports are anecdotal. However, I have had patients who say it has worked well for them.

Minerals

Our bodies need minerals in addition to vitamins. Why? Because many vitamins cannot be assimilated by the body without the help of minerals. Also, our bodies cannot make our own minerals. We must ingest them in a way our bodies can absorb so that they can do the vital work our body needs in order to remain healthy.

The body does not easily assimilate minerals. In order to assimilate minerals properly, our digestive system must be able to form chelates that the body can use. Since many people do not have an efficient digestive system that can form chelates, the mineral supplement they take may be eliminated without ever having been assimilated.

There are mineral supplements available today that are labeled "chelated." These supplements have undergone a process that has improved their potential for absorption. I highly recommend chelated mineral supplements for that reason.

Boron

NUTRIENT INFORMATION
- Boron helps reduce calcium excretion.
- It may retard bone loss in postmenopausal women.

BENEFITS FOR YOUR BODY
- Found to help in treatment of osteoarthritis
- Helpful in preventing osteoporosis
- Helpful in menopause by raising levels of estrogen in the blood
- Promotes healthy bones, teeth, hair and nails

BEST NATURAL SOURCES
- Apples, grapes, raisins, carrots

HOW TO SUPPLEMENT
- Take 3 mg. daily.

TOXICITY ISSUES
- Rare

DOCTOR'S COMMENTS
- If you have osteoporosis or are at risk for osteoporosis, taking 3 mg. of boron daily can be helpful to you by preventing loss of calcium and magnesium from your bones.

Calcium

NUTRIENT INFORMATION

- Calcium is the most abundant of all minerals used by the body and is required for healthy bones and teeth.
- Calcium is the mineral most often lacking in American women; 80 percent are estimated to be deficient in calcium.
- Calcium and magnesium are essential for a healthy cardiovascular system and proper heart rhythm.
- It plays an important role in regulation of blood pressure.
- To insure calcium absorption, the body must have sufficient vitamin D.

BENEFITS FOR YOUR BODY

- Maintains strong bones and healthy teeth
- Helps prevent osteoporosis
- May help prevent colon cancer
- Maintains regular heart rhythm and cardiovascular health
- Has a calming effect on the body, alleviates anxiety and prevents insomnia
- Helps lower blood pressure
- Helps relieve muscle spasms and leg cramps
- Helps relieve headaches caused by muscle tension
- May help alleviate menstrual cramps

BEST NATURAL SOURCES

- Milk (fat free), cheeses, salmon (include bones), green leafy vegetables (especially kale and collard greens), tofu, broccoli, yogurt (nonfat)

HOW TO SUPPLEMENT

- Calcium is usually found in 250–500 mg. tablets.
- Usual daily dose is 1,000–1,200 mg. per day. (Some doctors recommend that menopausal women take up to 1,500 mg. daily.)
- Postmenopausal women need about 1,500 mg. daily, as set by the National Institutes of Health.
- Do not take more than 2,500 mg. daily.
- It is best absorbed when taken with food and in divided doses of not more than 500 mg. each.
- The best form is a chelated calcium tablet. Calcium citrate is the most absorbable calcium and is also recommended for anyone who has a history of kidney stones.
- Calcium citrate is also available in an effervescent tablet that dissolves into a pleasant-tasting drink for those who have found it difficult to swallow large pills.
- Calcium should be taken with magnesium with a ratio of twice as much calcium as magnesium (2:1).
- Hydroxyapatite is a source of calcium made from powdered bovine bone. It is also easily absorbed by the body and contains other minerals such as magnesium, fluoride and potassium

EXCESS/LACK

- High calcium intake (over 2,500 mg.) may cause constipation and kidney stones.
- Lack of calcium can lead to osteoporosis, heart palpitations, aching joints, insomnia, muscle cramps and tooth decay.

TOXICITY ISSUES

- Rare

DOCTOR'S COMMENTS

- For insomnia, take a portion of your calcium supplement one-half hour before bedtime.

- If you consume a lot of caffeinated drinks or eat a high-protein diet, you are probably not absorbing calcium properly and need supplementation.
- Taking antacids as a source of calcium is not a good idea. Antacids have actually been shown to prevent the absorption of calcium.
- It is very difficult to obtain your total daily calcium requirement from food, so I recommend a good calcium supplement for everyone. It is best to find a supplement that combines calcium with magnesium.
- Children and teenagers who experience "growing pains" should increase calcium intake to diminish or eliminate the pains.
- In addition to a calcium supplement, all women should do some weight-bearing exercise weekly to prevent bone loss and help build bone.
- CAUTION: Some calcium supplements have been found to be contaminated with lead. Be careful to purchase your calcium from reputable sources.

Minerals

Chromium

NUTRIENT INFORMATION
- Chromium helps restore glucose tolerance in the body.
- It works closely with insulin to help metabolize sugar.
- It is essential for energy production.

BENEFITS FOR YOUR BODY
- Works to prevent or deter diabetes
- Helps prevent sudden drops in energy
- Helps regulate cholesterol levels
- Helps eliminate sugar cravings

BEST NATURAL SOURCES
- Wheat germ, brewer's yeast, chicken, brown rice

HOW TO SUPPLEMENT
- Chromium picolinate and chromium polynicotinate are the preferred forms.
- Usual dose is 100–200 mcg. daily.

EXCESS/LACK
- Deficiency may contribute to arteriosclerosis and diabetes.

TOXICITY ISSUES
- None known

DOCTOR'S COMMENTS
- People with diabetes who take chromium should do so under medical supervision. Their insulin dosage may need reduction as their blood sugar drops naturally from the effects of this supplement.

Copper

NUTRIENT INFORMATION

- Copper is necessary to convert iron into hemoglobin.
- It is essential for the utilization of vitamin C.
- Copper is found in a number of enzymes that contribute to the manufacture of collagen and are essential for the formation of bone and connective tissue.

BENEFITS FOR YOUR BODY

- It aids in effective iron absorption.
- It helps strengthen elastin in blood vessels.
- It helps support immune system.
- It helps body remove toxins and unwanted substances.
- It helps improve body's glucose tolerance.
- Proper zinc-copper ratio has been shown to help lower cholesterol.

BEST NATURAL SOURCES

- Almonds, broccoli, lentils, most seafood

HOW TO SUPPLEMENT

- Take 2 mg. daily (usually found in most multivitamins).

EXCESS/LACK

- Lack of copper in the body can lead to anemia, insomnia, hair loss, depression and osteoporosis.
- Inadequate copper levels may be linked to heart disease.

TOXICITY ISSUES

- Toxicity is rare.
- High doses may cause vomiting.

DOCTOR'S COMMENTS

- Special supplementation is rarely needed if you eat enough whole grains and leafy green vegetables.
- Copper and zinc levels must remain in balance; an excess of one produces a deficiency of the other. A general rule for balance would be 1 mg. copper to 10 mg. zinc.
- Cooking and storing acidic foods in copper pots help raise your intake of copper.

Iodine

NUTRIENT INFORMATION
- Iodine is vital to thyroid hormone synthesis.
- Two-thirds of the body's iodine is in the thyroid gland.
- Iodine is needed only in trace amounts.
- Our main source of iodine is in iodized salt.

BENEFITS FOR YOUR BODY
- Helps with dieting by burning excess fat
- Prevents hypothyroidism, which results in weight gain, mental slowness and fatigue
- Maintains healthy energy levels

BEST NATURAL SOURCES
- Sea kelp, clams, oysters, saltwater fish

HOW TO SUPPLEMENT
- Iodine is available in multimineral and high-potency vitamin supplements. The usual daily dose is 150 mcg.

EXCESS/LACK
- Both a deficiency of iodine and an excess of iodine limit the synthesis of thyroid hormone leading either to hypothyroidism (lack) or goiter (excess).

TOXICITY ISSUES
- Rare unless you consume excessive amounts of kelp or salt tablets

DOCTOR'S COMMENTS
- This is not a mineral that usually requires supplementation. However, if you live inland, far from the sea, where the soil may not contain iodine, be sure to use iodized salt.

Iron

NUTRIENT INFORMATION

- Iron is necessary for the production of hemoglobin (red blood corpuscles) and the oxygenation of red blood cells.
- Women's need for iron is higher than men's due to blood lost in the menstrual flow, especially in women who experience extremely heavy periods.
- Excessive amounts of zinc and vitamin E interfere with iron absorption, as does the high intake of caffeine.

BENEFITS FOR YOUR BODY

- Keeps immune system healthy
- Produces energy and prevents fatigue
- Cures and prevents iron-deficiency anemia

BEST NATURAL SOURCES

- Meat, poultry, nuts, beans, egg yolks, oysters, oatmeal, cauliflower, peas, broccoli, lima beans, asparagus, blackstrap molasses.

HOW TO SUPPLEMENT

- The best iron in supplement form is "acid chelate," which is organic iron that has been processed for rapid assimilation. This form will not cause constipation or stomach distress.
- Iron supplements come in a wide range of doses. I suggest you consult with a healthcare professional before taking an iron supplement.
- The recommended daily allowance according to the National Research Council is 10–15 mg. for adults.

EXCESS/LACK

- Iron deficiency is the most common nutrient deficiency in children.

- Iron deficiency is the most common nutritional cause of anemia.
- High levels of iron may be linked to heart disease, especially in men.

TOXICITY ISSUES

- Adult doses of iron can be toxic to children. Keep all iron supplements out of reach of children.
- CAUTION: If you have sickle-cell anemia, hemochromatosis or thalassemia, you should follow a professional medical treatment regimen.

DOCTOR'S COMMENTS

- I strongly recommend that you obtain your iron from plant sources and food. Iron supplements should be taken with care and only after consultation with a physician.
- I am against all iron supplementation unless prescribed by a physician.
- Anyone who believes they may be anemic should be diagnosed by a physician before self-medicating with iron. Some forms of iron are not highly absorbable and may have toxic side effects such as joint destruction, joint pain and swelling.
- Keep your iron supplements safely out of reach of children; they can be deadly to them!
- If you are pregnant, check with your doctor before taking iron.

Magnesium

NUTRIENT INFORMATION

- Magnesium is a powerful antioxidant.
- It is very important for nerve function.
- It is essential to the body's energy production.
- Magnesium is an important mineral to help prevent osteoporosis in women.

BENEFITS FOR YOUR BODY

- Helps the body burn fat
- Normalizes and increases energy levels
- Offers protection against cardiovascular disease and helps prevent heart attacks
- Helps prevent kidney stones
- Combined with calcium can have a calming influence on the body; can help with sleep
- May help lessen severity of asthma attacks
- Helps lessen symptoms of PMS, including breast tenderness, water retention and mood swings
- Helps prevent headaches
- Helps prevent muscle spasms and leg cramps
- Helps decrease pain of fibromyalgia

BEST NATURAL SOURCES

- Nuts, seeds, tofu, dark green vegetables, figs, bananas

HOW TO SUPPLEMENT

- Magnesium aspartate and magnesium citrate are the best forms for maximum absorption.
- Usual dose is 250–400 mg. daily; a safe upper limit is 750 mg. daily.

EXCESS/LACK

- Low levels of magnesium may cause heart irregularities, mental confusion, muscle cramps and insomnia.
- Magnesium levels are often low in diabetics and people with high blood pressure.
- Excess may cause diarrhea.

TOXICITY ISSUES

- People with kidney disease may not effectively excrete excess magnesium and can become toxic. Use only recommended doses.
- Toxicity symptoms include nausea, vomiting, difficulty in breathing and a low heart rate.

DOCTOR'S COMMENTS

- Many elderly people are deficient in magnesium. Other people who need magnesium supplementation include people who drink alcohol, women who use birth control pills and people who use diuretics.
- Magnesium is very important for anyone at risk of developing heart disease.
- Magnesium works best with vitamin A, calcium and phosphorus. For every 250 mg. of magnesium take 500 mg. of calcium: a ratio of 2:1.

Minerals

Manganese

NUTRIENT INFORMATION

- Manganese is an antioxidant mineral.
- It is essential in the formation of many enzymes and hormones, including thyroxin from the thyroid gland.
- Manganese helps support normal metabolism.
- It supports healthy bones.

BENEFITS FOR YOUR BODY

- Helps normalize energy levels; eliminates fatigue
- Aids in muscle reflexes; helpful for carpal tunnel syndrome
- Reduces nervousness and irritability
- Helps regulate glucose tolerance

BEST NATURAL SOURCES

- Whole grains, avocados, wheat germ, nuts, shellfish

HOW TO SUPPLEMENT

- Usual dose is 2–5 mg. daily.
- A safe upper limit is 10 mg.

EXCESS/LACK

- Too much manganese can interfere with the body's absorption of iron.
- High doses cause loss of motor function similar to Parkinson's symptoms.

TOXICITY ISSUES

- Toxicity is very rare.

DOCTOR'S COMMENTS

- Manganese helps break down carbohydrates and fats for energy, so if you suffer from fatigue, check to see if your multiple vitamin supplement includes manganese.

Potassium

NUTRIENT INFORMATION

- Potassium is important for a regular heart rhythm.
- It is essential for cell health and a healthy nervous system.
- In conjunction with sodium, it assists in regulating the water balance in the body.
- Stress, diarrhea and low blood sugar can cause potassium loss.

BENEFITS FOR YOUR BODY

- Helps send oxygen to the brain; prevents stroke
- Aids in energy production
- Aids in reducing high blood pressure
- Helps normalize heart rhythms
- Helps prevent leg cramps and muscle spasms
- Alleviates pain of sciatica

BEST NATURAL SOURCES

- Bananas, apricots, cantaloupe, all green leafy vegetables, fish, potatoes, blackstrap molasses

HOW TO SUPPLEMENT

- Found in most quality multivitamin and multimineral products
- Can be purchased separately as potassium gluconate, potassium citrate or potassium chloride
- Usual dose: 2,000–3,500 mg. daily

EXCESS/LACK

- Deficiency can lead to cramping, fatigue, irregular heart beat, salt retention and edema.
- Excess can cause irregular heartbeat.

Minerals

TOXICITY ISSUES

- Rare, because excess is excreted in the urine. However, anyone with kidney disease should avoid high doses.

DOCTOR'S COMMENTS

- If you drink a lot of coffee, drink alcohol or take diuretics, you are probably low in potassium.
- Stress increases the body's need for potassium.
- CAUTION: People with kidney disorders should not take potassium supplements since excess potassium needs to be excreted by the kidneys.

Selenium

NUTRIENT INFORMATION

- Selenium is a potent antioxidant.
- It helps neutralize free radicals that cause damage to the body's tissues and arteries.
- Vitamin E and selenium are more effective when taken together than when they are taken individually.
- Men have an increased need for selenium because it is expelled in their semen.

BENEFITS FOR YOUR BODY

- May greatly reduce risk of cancer, especially lung, prostate, colon and skin cancers
- May reduce risk of heart disease and stroke
- Prevents age and liver spots
- Helps fight bacterial infections
- May help raise sperm count

BEST NATURAL SOURCES

- Garlic, onions, red grapes, brown rice, tuna, liver, broccoli (dependent upon the selenium content in the soil where product is grown)

HOW TO SUPPLEMENT

- Usual dose: 100–200 mcg. daily
- Can often be found combined with vitamin E

EXCESS/LACK

- Deficiency has been linked to cancer and heart disease.
- Excess can cause a metallic taste in the mouth and garlic breath odor.

TOXICITY ISSUES

- Extremely high doses can be toxic to liver and kidney function, but this is rare.
- To avoid toxicity your intake should not exceed 400 mcg. daily.

DOCTOR'S COMMENTS

- I advocate taking a selenium supplement due to its powerful antioxidant and anticancer properties. Also, selenium levels in our bodies decrease with age.
- Much of our soil is "mineral depleted," so you may not be getting adequate doses from your food.
- Any man over fifty years of age should add selenium to his daily regimen to protect against prostate enlargement and cancer.

Vanadium

NUTRIENT INFORMATION

- Vanadium mimics the action of insulin in the body.
- It is essential for healthy bones, teeth, hair and nails.
- Vanadium helps inhibit cholesterol buildup in blood vessels.
- It plays an important role in reproduction.

BENEFITS FOR YOUR BODY

- Effective in normalizing blood sugar levels
- Helps control insulin-resistant and Type II diabetes
- May possibly stimulate muscle growth, increasing muscle size and strength
- Helps body remove toxins and harmful substances

BEST NATURAL SOURCES

- All fish, olives, dill

HOW TO SUPPLEMENT

- For bodybuilding, usual dose is 10 mg. taken a half hour before working out.
- In recent studies a dose of 50 mg. once or twice daily was used effectively for persons with diabetes.
- CAUTION: Diabetics should check with their doctor for specific dosage.

EXCESS/LACK

- Deficiency can lead to kidney disease and problems with reproduction.
- Some people experience diarrhea or gastrointestinal upset at higher doses.

TOXICITY ISSUES

■ None known

DOCTOR'S COMMENTS

■ Most people do not need supplemental vanadium.

■ Although physicians who prescribe alternative medicine therapies use vanadium in the treatment of diabetes, I do not recommend that you try to self-medicate if you have diabetes or hypoglycemia. An improper dose of vanadium can possibly lower blood sugar levels too quickly, so supervision is imperative. Please consult your physician.

Zinc

NUTRIENT INFORMATION

- Zinc is required for protein synthesis as well as for collagen formation.
- It is important to your skin's utilization of vitamin A.
- It contributes to macular health of eyes.
- Zinc helps control inflammation.
- It helps adrenal glands manufacture hormones.
- It may have a function in maintaining sexual energy.
- It is important in prostate gland function.

BENEFITS FOR YOUR BODY

- Zinc promotes a healthy immune system.
- It aids in the treatment of acne and skin infections.
- Zinc lozenges can relieve a sore throat.
- It may reduce symptoms of macular degeneration of eye.
- It may help tinnitus (ringing in ears).
- It promotes wound healing.
- It maintains a healthy prostate.
- It aids in healthy sperm production.
- It helps treat mental disorders.

BEST NATURAL SOURCES

- Liver, eggs, seafood, wheat germ, pumpkinseeds, lima beans

HOW TO SUPPLEMENT

- Zinc is available in most multivitamin/multimineral supplements.
- Usual dose is 15–45 mg. per day.
- Zinc and copper ratios need to be maintained. Recommended ratio is 3 mg. copper to 45 mg. of zinc.

EXCESS/LACK

- Zinc deficiency may lead to benign prostatic hypertrophy (enlarged prostate), loss of taste and smell, and white spots on fingernails.
- Excessive zinc can produce a zinc/copper imbalance.

TOXICITY ISSUES

- Do not take more than 45 mg. per day. Higher doses (up to 100 mg. per day) can lead to immune system suppression and a high risk of infections.

DOCTOR'S COMMENTS

- Some studies in the United States and in Europe have shown that Alzheimer's patients may improve after taking supplemental zinc. I encourage elderly people to be sure they get enough zinc in order to avoid mental deterioration or dementia.
- One-fourth to one-half cup of raw pumpkinseeds daily can help prevent prostate enlargement and prostate infections.
- Liquid zinc may help cure anorexia. Consult your physician for details.

Amino Acids

Amino acids are building blocks that make up proteins. Because protein is the second largest component of our body weight, it is extremely important that we have sufficient protein intake for optimum health. Proteins are a necessary part of every cell of our body.

Chains of amino acids linked together make proteins that form various kinds of tissues with unique functions and characteristics. The proteins we eat must be broken down by the body into the various amino acids to be utilized to build healthy bodies.

Vitamins and minerals also cannot perform their jobs effectively without the help of specific amino acids. If even one essential amino acid is missing, the body will not be able to utilize protein properly.

It is not wise to eat excessive amounts of protein in order to get more amino acids into your body. And lifestyle factors such as stress and trauma can contribute to deficiencies of amino acids that we do get from our diets. Also, if you prefer to eat as a vegetarian, a formula containing all essential amino acids will ensure that your protein requirements are met.

Creatine

Amino Acids

NUTRIENT INFORMATION

- Creatine is a nutrient that is found naturally in the body and is produced from a combination of three amino acids: arginine, glycine and methionine.
- Creatine helps the body produce fuel for cellular activity.
- It is used mainly by bodybuilders and athletes to improve strength, stamina and muscle mass.
- The creatine in the body is concentrated in the skeletal muscles and provides the energy the muscles need to move.
- Vegetarians have lower levels of creatine than meat eaters do.

BENEFITS FOR YOUR BODY

- Helps you to gain body strength
- Builds lean muscle mass
- Boosts energy
- Helps reduce body fat
- May help lower total cholesterol and triglycerides

BEST NATURAL SOURCES

- Tuna, salmon, beef, pork, cod

HOW TO SUPPLEMENT

- Creatine is available as a capsule or in powdered form to be mixed with water or juice.
- Supplementation is usually divided into two phases: the loading phase, which lasts from five to seven days, and the maintenance phase, which continues for an extended period of time.
- Doses are based on body weight; charts are generally supplied with the supplement.

- Usual dose is 12–20 grams daily for loading, 4–12 grams daily for maintenance.

EXCESS/LACK
- No side effects are reported with suggested doses.
- Excess may cause diarrhea and/or nausea.

TOXICITY ISSUES
- None known

DOCTOR'S COMMENTS
- If you have any medical problems, especially a kidney disorder, please consult your physician before taking creatine.
- Some studies have shown that 3 grams of creatine daily for twenty-eight days may be effective for older people to increase strength and muscle, rather than using the loading and maintenance doses used by athletes and bodybuilders.

Amino Acids

Glutathione

NUTRIENT INFORMATION

- Glutathione is one of the body's primary and most important antioxidants to help protect against free-radical damage.
- It converts fat-soluble heavy metals and toxins into water-soluble waste, which can be excreted by the kidneys.
- Glutathione is essential for liver detoxification.
- It is found in virtually every cell in the body as well as in the fluid that surrounds the lens of the eye.

BENEFITS FOR YOUR BODY

- Enhances immune system
- Enhances brain function
- May offer protection against Alzheimer's disease
- Believed to have strong antiaging benefits
- May reduce progression of arthritis
- Protects eyes against disease

BEST NATURAL SOURCES

- To help the body produce glutathione you need to eat foods containing sulfur, such as eggs, garlic and onions.

HOW TO SUPPLEMENT

- Usual dose is 50–100 mg. once or twice a day.

EXCESS/LACK

- Appears safe even at high doses

TOXICITY ISSUES

- None known

DOCTOR'S COMMENTS

- Glutathione is essential for two very important areas of

health: your liver and your eyes.

- Studies have shown that people who are ill usually have low levels of glutathione.
- Healthy older people have very high levels of glutathione.
- Three supplements that help your body produce glutathione are:
  - Alpha lipoic acid (page 82)
  - N-acetylcysteine (NAC) (page 75)
  - Milk thistle (page 127)

L-Arginine

NUTRIENT INFORMATION

- L-arginine is an amino acid that is necessary for the release of the growth hormone from the pituitary gland.
- It is involved in production of nitric oxide, which helps the male achieve an erection.
- L-arginine also plays a role in the health of the cardiovascular system, the immune system and blood pressure.

BENEFITS FOR YOUR BODY

- Helps stimulate production of growth hormone
- A vasodilator, thereby helping to lower blood pressure
- Helps increase blood flow to the penis
- Helps men have firmer erections
- Helps increase sperm count
- May help the body fight cancer and tumors
- Promotes wound healing
- Promotes physical and mental alertness
- Boosts immune response by stimulating T cells, the body's natural guards against bacteria and viruses
- Helps the body shed fat and build and tone muscle
- Guards against heart disease by preventing formation of plaque

BEST NATURAL SOURCES

- Chocolate, nuts, sunflower seeds, sesame seeds, raisins, soybeans, protein-rich foods.

HOW TO SUPPLEMENT

- Usual dose is 1 gram, three times per day.
- It should be taken on an empty stomach.
- It is also sold in powdered form that can be mixed with water.

- To use for muscle toning, take 2 grams one hour prior to exercise.
- For enhanced sexual function, take 3 grams prior to sexual activity.

EXCESS/LACK

- Deficiency may lead to low sperm count.
- Excess may trigger herpes outbreaks in people with the herpes virus.

TOXICITY ISSUES

- Extremely high doses could cause bone deformities.

DOCTOR'S COMMENTS

- This supplement shows a good deal of promise for treatment of erectile dysfunction. To date, anecdotal reports of its success have been documented quite frequently in medical literature.
- I do not recommend giving L-arginine to growing children because it may have an adverse effect on their bones.

Amino Acids

65

L-Carnitine

NUTRIENT INFORMATION

- L-carnitine is essential for normal fat/energy metabolism; it helps convert fatty acids to energy.
- People with heart disease are often found to be deficient in this important nutrient.

BENEFITS FOR YOUR BODY

- Increases fat metabolism
- Improves angina
- Lowers LDL (bad) cholesterol levels and boosts HDL (good) cholesterol levels
- May enhance physical stamina during workouts and athletic performance
- May improve memory in the elderly
- May slow progression of Alzheimer's disease according to some European studies

BEST NATURAL SOURCES

- Red meat, fish, milk
- Good vegetarian source: soy tempeh

HOW TO SUPPLEMENT

- Usual dose is 500 mg. twice daily.
- Take one-half hour before eating or two hours after eating.

EXCESS/LACK

- Extreme excess may cause body to develop a "fishy" odor, which can be corrected simply by cutting back on your dosage.

Amino Acids

TOXICITY ISSUES

- Toxicity is rare.
- CAUTION: If you have a heart condition, consult your physician before adding this supplement to your regimen.

DOCTOR'S COMMENTS

- This is a rather expensive supplement, but if you have angina or elevated cholesterol levels it is well worth trying.
- Use L-carnitine or acetyl-carnitine forms instead of D-carnitine. Some studies have suggested that D-carnitine may cause some toxicity.

L-Glutamine

Amino Acids

NUTRIENT INFORMATION

- L-glutamine is converted into glutamic acid in the body, which is a vital brain nutrient.
- L-glutamine is a component of glutathione, the body's most essential amino acid. If you are low in L-glutamine, you probably have a deficiency of glutathione as well.
- It is a natural agent for releasing growth hormone.

BENEFITS FOR YOUR BODY

- Improves memory and mental clarity
- Combats fatigue
- Helps stop alcohol and sugar cravings
- Prevents muscle degeneration, especially in the elderly or people with chronic illness
- Helps strengthen immune system
- Helps body lose fat and maintain muscle

BEST NATURAL SOURCES

- Protein-rich foods like chicken, tuna, turkey, fish, egg whites

HOW TO SUPPLEMENT

- Usual dose is 2 to 10 grams daily.
- Bodybuilders will often use 5 to 20 grams per day to increase muscle mass and fat-burning.

EXCESS/LACK

- Should not be given to children on a regular basis as it is a brain stimulant. Excess may cause a feeling of over-stimulation.

TOXICITY ISSUES

- Some people may be allergic to extremely high doses.

DOCTOR'S COMMENTS

■ L-glutamine is essential for a healthy brain and a strong immune system. Many "baby boomers" are lacking sufficient amino acids because they have eliminated protein intake as a result of constant dieting. If you have eliminated beef and pork, try to add protein to your diet from other sources or try supplementing with amino acids.

L-Phenylalanine

NUTRIENT INFORMATION
- Phenylalanine is required for release of the growth hormone from the pituitary gland.
- Without phenylalanine, the brain cannot release dopamine and norepinephrine, which are natural antidepressants.

BENEFITS FOR YOUR BODY
- Acts as a natural appetite suppressant
- May act as an effective mood elevator and antidepressant
- Increases sexual interest
- Promotes alertness
- Enhances memory
- May alleviate migraine headaches according to clinical trials
- May be of use in treating Parkinson's disease by increasing dopamine levels

BEST NATURAL SOURCES
- Cottage cheese, almonds, soy products, pumpkinseeds, sesame seeds

HOW TO SUPPLEMENT
- To suppress appetite, take 250–500 mg. one hour before meals.
- For energy, take 250–500 mg. between meals.

EXCESS/LACK
- Deficiency can contribute to depression.

TOXICITY ISSUES
- Do not take phenylalanine if you have high blood pressure.

- Do not take phenylalanine it you use an MAO inhibitor or take other antidepressant drugs.
- Do not take phenylalanine if you have melanoma or are pregnant.

 DOCTOR'S COMMENTS

- There is another form of this amino acid called DL-phenylalanine or DLPA. This is a combination of D–phenylalanine (synthetic form) and L–phenylalanine (natural form). This has been tested as a painkiller and in some studies has been found to be highly effective in providing relief for chronic pain by increasing the body's natural endorphin level. It is nonaddictive.

L-Tyrosine

NUTRIENT INFORMATION
- L-tyrosine increases the rate at which the brain produces dopamine and norepinephrine (natural antidepressants).
- Some prescription medications for depression work by boosting L-tyrosine levels in the brain.
- L-tyrosine has been found to be very effective in helping cocaine addicts quit using cocaine.
- It is essential for normal thyroid hormone production.

BENEFITS FOR YOUR BODY
- Effectively treats depression without side effects
- Improves mood and mental function
- Improves sex drive by increasing dopamine levels
- Suppresses appetite
- Helps increase muscle growth and reduce body fat
- Helps counteract the effects of stress on the body
- May help trigger the release of the growth hormone from the pituitary gland

BEST NATURAL SOURCES
- Meat, wheat

HOW TO SUPPLEMENT
- 1,000 mg. twice daily one-half hour before meals

EXCESS/LACK
- Excess may cause a feeling of being overstimulated.

TOXICITY
- Do not use L-tyrosine if you have high blood pressure, have melanoma, take a MAO inhibitor or take other antidepressant drugs.

DOCTOR'S COMMENTS

■ If you are taking antidepressants, you may want to consult your physician to see about taking L-tyrosine, which is a natural antidepressant, for a trial period instead of your other medication.

Lysine

 NUTRIENT INFORMATION
- Lysine is an essential amino acid that is not manufactured in the body; it must be obtained through diet or supplementation.
- It assists in the formation of antibodies and enzymes.
- Lysine assists in the formation of collagen.
- It aids the body in the efficient use of calcium.

 BENEFITS FOR YOUR BODY
- May reduce symptoms and prevent recurrence of herpes
- Aids in treatment of canker and cold sores
- Promotes bone health; hence may help prevent osteoporosis
- Helps keep skin healthy and firm

 BEST NATURAL SOURCES
- Meat, fish, milk, cheese

 HOW TO SUPPLEMENT
- Usual dose is 500–1,000 mg. daily (one-half hour before meals).

 EXCESS/LACK
- Lack of lysine can lead to hair loss, anemia and fatigue.
- Vegetarians may be prone to lysine deficiency.

 TOXICITY ISSUES
- None known

 DOCTOR'S COMMENTS
- Some researchers believe that L-arginine (page 64) triggers herpes outbreaks. If you are taking L-arginine, you can counteract this negative effect by taking 500 mg. of lysine daily.

N-Acetylcysteine
(NAC)

NUTRIENT INFORMATION

- NAC is a sulfur-containing amino acid that is a precursor to glutathione, a powerful natural antioxidant that helps reduce free radicals in the blood.
- It is helpful in breaking down mucus in the lungs and sinuses.
- It may help protect the body from heavy metal toxicity.

BENEFITS FOR YOUR BODY

- Repairs damage done to the body and lungs by smoke or smoking
- Prevents respiratory diseases (bronchitis, asthma, emphysema)
- Boosts immune function
- May help heal ear infections
- Promotes healing of sinus infections

HOW TO SUPPLEMENT

- Usual dose is 500 mg. one to three times daily.

TOXICITY ISSUES

- Do not use if you have a history of ulcers or gastroenteritis

DOCTOR'S COMMENTS

- I know of some practitioners who recommend NAC for treatment of flu symptoms as it helps detoxify the body and supports the immune system.

Taurine

NUTRIENT INFORMATION
- Taurine is the primary building block for other amino acids.
- Your body is able to synthesize taurine on its own.
- It is necessary for heart tissue, white blood cells, skeletal muscles and central nervous system.
- Taurine supports brain function.

BENEFITS FOR YOUR BODY
- Strengthens heart function and heart muscle
- May prevent heart failure in people with heart disease
- Helps prevent macular degeneration
- Aids in treatment of anxiety, epilepsy and hyperactivity

BEST NATURAL SOURCES
- Meat, dairy, eggs, fish

HOW TO SUPPLEMENT
- Taurine is available in 500-mg. capsules.
- Take 500-mg. tablet two to three times daily one-half hour before meals.

EXCESS/LACK
- Vegetarians are more likely to have low levels of taurine.

TOXICITY ISSUES
- Rare

DOCTOR'S COMMENTS
- Although many naturopathic doctors treat heart disease by using taurine, I want to remind you not to self-medicate if you have a heart condition. Please consult your physician about using this supplement.

Other Natural Supplements

In this section I have presented many natural supplements that are suitable for treating specific conditions. These interesting nutritional supplements are also helpful to prevent the occurrence of disease conditions. Each is briefly explained with many of the benefits for your body listed so that you will understand better why you should add them to your nutritional regimen.

I have tried to make simplicity the rule to help you choose wisely the most important supplements that you and your loved ones should consider using for optimum health. With these reference tools, you can make intelligent decisions about how to improve your health and prevent future illness.

Acidophilus/ Probiotics

NUTRIENT INFORMATION

- Probiotic means "favoring life." It is a term used to describe friendly, beneficial bacteria that are normal inhabitants of the large and small intestines.
- Probiotics boost the body's own defense against disease, attaching to the walls of the colon to help establish a healthy balance of bacteria.
- There are two categories of probiotics: lactobacillus acidophilus and bifidobacterium bifidum.

BENEFITS FOR YOUR BODY

- Aid in digestion and absorption of nutrients
- Protect body from harmful infections, fungi and parasites
- Prevent recurrent yeast infections (candida albicans)
- Inhibit growth of salmonella and E-coli
- Prevent and treat urinary tract infections
- Improve lactose tolerance (by helping to produce lactase)
- Have anticancer properties
- Support the immune system
- Helpful in treatment of bowel disorders and digestive problems, including diarrhea, gas and bad breath
- Help prevent food allergies

BEST NATURAL SOURCES

- Yogurt made with live, active culture
- Note: If allergic to cows' milk, look for soy or goat's milk yogurt

Supplements

78

HOW TO SUPPLEMENT

- Usual dose: three capsules daily (containing at least one billion organisms per capsule) taken with a large glass of water
- Also sold in liquids and powders, which are usually more potent and need to be refrigerated
- May cause a bloated feeling at first, which is normal and will pass

EXCESS/LACK

- Lack may lead to constipation or elimination problems.

TOXICITY ISSUES

- None known

DOCTOR'S COMMENTS

- When using an antibiotic, it is very important to take probiotics during the time you are taking the prescription drug and for two to four weeks following the antibiotic treatment. This is because antibiotics cannot tell the difference between healthful and harmful bacteria, so they kill the good bacteria as well as the bad.
- Without our good bacteria to protect us, our bodies are susceptible to many unhealthy pathogens, which can severely compromise our immune system.

Supplements

Aloe Vera

- Aloe vera may be the single most healing source of all the herbs.
- The aloe leaf is filled with 96 percent water, but the other 4 percent contains seventy-five known healing substances, including amino acids, vitamins, minerals and enzymes.
- Aloe vera also contains antibacterial and antifungal properties.
- The aloe gel is a mild anesthetic as well.

BENEFITS FOR YOUR BODY

- Aids in healing of intestinal problems, including diarrhea, constipation, ulcers and colitis
- Powerfully stimulates the immune system, including T4 fighter cells, the body's natural guards against bacteria and viruses
- Reduces fasting blood sugar in diabetics
- Reduces inflammation of arthritis
- Stimulates immune response against cancer
- Reduces cholesterol and triglycerides
- Can protect skin from radiation damage when applied topically
- May have a positive effect in the treatment of the HIV virus
- May help repair DNA
- Helps reduce psoriasis symptoms
- Speeds wound healing
- Soothes burns
- Dilates capillaries, increasing circulation
- A natural colon cleanser

Supplements

BEST NATURAL SOURCES
- Fresh leaf or juice of aloe vera plant

HOW TO SUPPLEMENT
- Usual dose for capsule form: 500–1,000 mg. daily
- Usual dose for liquid form: 2–6 mg. per day (depending on state of health)

TOXICITY ISSUES
- None known
- Safe even at high doses

DOCTOR'S COMMENTS
- The testimonials I have received from patients regarding the healing properties of aloe vera are amazing. I am still astonished at how much this little plant can do!
- Look for cold-pressed aloe vera when buying a liquid as heat can break down the large saccharide chains, which are believed to contribute to healing.
- CAUTION: There are many aloe vera products on the market that actually contain very little of the herb itself, or they may contain "aloe extract." Be sure that your product ingredients list aloe vera as the primary ingredient or assures you that it is at least 95 percent pure aloe vera.

Supplements

Alpha Lipoic Acid

NUTRIENT INFORMATION

- Alpha lipoic acid is an important antioxidant that boosts the power of other antioxidants, especially vitamins C and E.
- It also raises glutathione levels in the body.
- It is the only antioxidant that is both water and fat soluble, so it protects all areas of the body.
- It helps protect cell membranes.
- It has an insulin-like effect on the body.

BENEFITS FOR YOUR BODY

- Helpful in treatment of diabetes by assisting in normalizing blood sugar
- Aids in treatment of glaucoma
- Aids in treatment of diabetic peripheral neuropathy
- May prevent cataracts
- May help improve memory
- Helps improve HDL:LDL ratio (cholesterol)
- Protects against cancer and heart disease
- Helpful in people with chronic asthma
- Helps support and detoxify the liver

BEST NATURAL SOURCES

- Red meat, yeast, potatoes

HOW TO SUPPLEMENT

- Usual dose is 200–600 mg. daily.
- It is difficult to obtain enough via diet.

TOXICITY ISSUES

- None known

DOCTOR'S COMMENTS

- More and more studies are confirming the value of this powerful antioxidant supplement.
- This nutrient has been advised for use by anyone at risk for cataracts or glaucoma (take in addition to lutein and bilberry).
- Alpha lipoic acid can also help reduce elevated blood sugar levels in diabetics and reduce nerve damage caused by diabetes.
- It is not for use during pregnancy until further studies are done.

Androstenedione

NUTRIENT INFORMATION

- Androstenedione is a metabolite of DHEA, which is a hormone that occurs naturally in the human body.
- It is believed to be an over-the-counter testosterone booster.
- It has been widely publicized for its use by sports figures.

BENEFITS FOR YOUR BODY

- May help boost testosterone levels

BEST NATURAL SOURCES

- Dietary supplement

HOW TO SUPPLEMENT

- Usual dose for men is 100 mg. twice daily.
- Usual dose for women is 50 mg. daily.
- It is recommended to use androstenedione supplement in the following cycle: Use for three to four weeks; take one to three weeks off.

EXCESS/LACK

- Excess can result in facial hair growth and acne in women.

TOXICITY ISSUES

- None reported

DOCTOR'S COMMENTS

- Do not use this (or any testosterone-boosting product) if you have any history of a prostate disorder.
- Androstenedione can raise unwanted estrogen levels in women, so women who want to boost their testosterone levels would do better to consider using 4-androstenedione (4-ADIOL), which does not convert to estrogen.

- CAUTION: I do not advise using this supplement without consulting your physician first because medical literature does not contain sufficient long-term studies.

Avena Sativa

NUTRIENT INFORMATION
- Avena sativa is derived from the green leaves of the "wild oat" plant.
- Researchers believe it gradually raises the testosterone level in men.

BENEFITS FOR YOUR BODY
- Raises libido (increases interest in sex)
- Enhances sexual endurance
- Enhances strength of orgasms
- May help reduce cravings for sweets

BEST NATURAL SOURCES
- Natural herb

HOW TO SUPPLEMENT
- Usual dose is 750 mg.
- Take three doses daily for about two months, then decrease to one to two daily depending upon results.

TOXICITY ISSUES
- None known

DOCTOR'S COMMENTS

- Whoever first used the phrase "sowing your wild oats" may have been thinking of avena sativa, which comes from green leaves of the wild oat plant, because this expression has been associated with the sexual vigor of youth for centuries.
- According to many of my patients, avena sativa is very helpful in raising levels of sexual desire.
- It does not work for everyone, of course, but there is enough evidence to make it worth trying!
- Men seem to notice slightly greater improvement than women do.

Beta-Glucan

NUTRIENT INFORMATION

- Beta-glucan is a potent immune enhancer.
- It modulates the body's immune system by activating the macrophages (large white immune cells). These immune cells can then recognize and destroy toxins, bacteria, viruses, fungi and parasites.

BENEFITS FOR YOUR BODY

- Activates and boosts the body's immune response
- Aids the body in fighting cancer
- Helps protect the body from negative effects of chemotherapy and radiation
- Prevents and reduces symptoms of cold and flu
- Prevents and speeds healing of pneumonia and strep throat

Supplements

- Treats fungi and parasites
- Relieves allergies and asthma
- May help relieve fibromyalgia and chronic fatigue syndrome

 ### BEST NATURAL SOURCES
- Derived from the cell wall of purified baker's yeast (will not give you a yeast infection).

 ### HOW TO SUPPLEMENT
- Usual dose is 3–6 mg. daily.
- Dosage may be increased to 10–40 mg. if immune system is already compromised by a disease process.

 ### TOXICITY ISSUES
- None known

 ### DOCTOR'S COMMENTS
- After reading the literature about beta-glucan's amazing effect on the immune system, I personally used beta-glucan during and after an upper respiratory illness and found it most effective to help shorten the recovery time.[1]
- When I interviewed Frank Jordan on *Doctor to Doctor*, he told me that research ranging from the U.S. military to the most prestigious medical schools indicated tumor reduction and lesion elimination in many forms of cancer.[2]

Bilberry

NUTRIENT INFORMATION

- Bilberry is a European blueberry that contains flavonoids, which are potent antioxidants.
- It protects the capillaries and improves blood flow to the eye.
- Bilberry helps to control insulin levels in the body.
- It has an interesting history of use, including World War II pilots in the Royal Air Force (RAF) who took bilberry to support and improve night vision.

BENEFITS FOR YOUR BODY

- May help halt or prevent macular degeneration of eyes
- Improves nighttime vision and may reverse night blindness
- Helps treat cataracts
- Helpful for retinitis pigmentosa of eyes
- For diabetes, aids in reduction of retinopathy
- Also has diuretic properties

BEST NATURAL SOURCES

- Natural herb

HOW TO SUPPLEMENT

- Usual dose is 80–160 mg. three times daily.

EXCESS/LACK

- Excess may lead to increased urination.

TOXICITY ISSUES

- None known

DOCTOR'S COMMENTS

- All the doctors who have been on our *Doctor to Doctor* television program discussing eye health have recommended supplementing with bilberry (or a product that contains bilberry) and lutein to prevent losing or compromising our sight as we age. Let's take heed and follow their advice!

Black Cohosh

NUTRIENT INFORMATION

- Black cohosh is an herbal plant that is high in phytoestrogens.
- It has a long tradition of use in folk healing.
- Studies have supported this herb's ability to balance hormones.

BENEFITS FOR YOUR BODY

- Helps diminish menopausal symptoms, including hot flashes, irritability and insomnia
- Helps diminish PMS symptoms
- Helps relieve menstrual cramps by relaxing the uterus
- May help restore regular menstrual cycles

BEST NATURAL SOURCES

- Natural herb

HOW TO SUPPLEMENT

- Black cohosh is often found in varying doses in women's PMS and menopause formulas combined with black licorice, chasteberry and dong quai, which have similar phytoestrogenic properties.

Supplements

89

EXCESS/LACK

- Too high doses can cause abdominal pain, dizziness, headaches and nausea.

TOXICITY ISSUES

- Side effects are rare when used at recommended doses.

DOCTOR'S COMMENTS

- Because this herb helps relax the uterus, do not use during pregnancy as it may facilitate premature labor.

Chondroitin

NUTRIENT INFORMATION

- Chondroitin is a naturally occurring substance found in high concentrations in connective tissue around the joints of the body.
- It draws fluid to joint cells and helps produce lubrication to allow smooth movement of the joint.
- People who suffer with arthritis have low levels of chondroitin.

BENEFITS FOR YOUR BODY

- Relieves and reverses symptoms of osteoarthritis and rheumatoid arthritis
- Stimulates the production of new cartilage
- Decrease arthritis pain
- Increases joint mobility
- Note: Works best in combination with glucosamine (page 108)

BEST NATURAL SOURCES
- Meat, especially near the joints

HOW TO SUPPLEMENT
- Usual dose: 1,200 mg. per day in divided doses
- Best when taken with glucosamine in a ratio of 5:4 (1,500 mg. glucosamine, 1,200 mg. chondroitin)

EXCESS/LACK
- People with arthritis have been found to have extremely low levels of chondroitin.

TOXICITY ISSUES
- None known

DOCTOR COMMENTS
- If you are using NSAIDs to control arthritis pain, please give chondroitin a try. NSAIDs have been the cause of approximately 15,000 deaths per year due to gastrointestinal ulcers and bleeding. In addition, it has been reported that about 25 percent of individuals who use NSAIDs regularly develop ulcers.[3]

Coenzyme Q-10

NUTRIENT INFORMATION

- Coenzyme Q-10, or COQ-10, is a powerful substance that enhances the activity of other enzymes.
- COQ-10 is used around the world as an antioxidant and a powerful heart protector.
- It is essential for the body to burn fat.
- It helps the body turn oxygen into energy that cells need for life.
- It helps increase oxygen flow to the heart.
- It works in the mitochondria (energy centers) of the cells.
- COQ-10 levels in the body are believed to decline with age.

BENEFITS FOR YOUR BODY

- Strengthens and protects the heart against cardiovascular disorders and heart disease, including arrhythmias
- Helps normalize blood pressure
- Reduces inflammation of fibromyalgia
- May assist in prevention and treatment of periodontal disease
- Improves energy levels for people with chronic fatigue syndrome
- Boosts immune system
- Improves angina
- Improves CHF (congestive heart failure)
- Helps with weight loss (has thermogenic properties)
- May help reduce breast tumors
- Helps decrease the fasting blood sugar in diabetics
- Helps control asthma

- Increases energy levels
- May help tinnitus (ringing in the ears)

BEST NATURAL SOURCES
- Fish, eggs, spinach, red meat

HOW TO SUPPLEMENT
- Usual dose is 60–90 mg. daily.
- For heart problems, increase dose to 180–360 mg. per day.

EXCESS/LACK
- Older people usually have lower levels of COQ-10.

TOXICITY ISSUES
- None known

DOCTOR'S COMMENTS
- Because scientific studies have documented coenzyme Q–10 as having so many powerful benefits, I highly recommend it on your list of "must-take" supplements. It is somewhat expensive, but the benefits for your heart alone make it worth every penny.
- CAUTION: According to some reports COQ-10 may decrease an individual's response to Coumadin (a blood-thinning drug). Consult your physician before using COQ-10 if you already take drugs for congestive heart failure or bleeding disorders.

DHEA
(Dehydroepiandrosterone)

 ### NUTRIENT INFORMATION
- DHEA is called the "mother" hormone.
- It is made by the adrenal glands and is converted into male hormones (androgens) and female hormones. In men, it breaks down further into testosterone.
- DHEA is found in high concentrations in the brain and controls the action of stress hormones (cortisol) on the body.
- It helps stabilize blood glucose levels.
- Levels of this "mother" hormone decrease substantially in the body with age. Declining levels are believed to be associated with age-related diseases such as arthritis, memory loss and heart disease.

 ### BENEFITS FOR YOUR BODY
- Relieves stress
- Improves memory
- Improves mood
- Relieves feelings of depression
- Improves libido; helps raise testosterone level in men as well as women
- Increases muscle strength and lean body mass
- Increases stamina and energy; helps chronic fatigue syndrome
- Appears to stimulate the production of immune cells as well as natural killer cells that fight cancer
- May have a positive effect on lupus and rheumatoid arthritis
- May be helpful in weight loss by stabilizing blood sugar levels and/or suppressing appetite

- May have a positive effect on senility and on Alzheimer's disease
- Helps protect against blood clot formation

BEST NATURAL SOURCES
- Dietary supplement made from sterols extracted from wild yams and converted to DHEA in the laboratory

HOW TO SUPPLEMENT
- Recommended dose is 5–25 mg. daily.
- Start with the lowest dose and increase by increments of 5–10 mg.
- Some experts suggest that men should take 50 mg. per day, but I think 25 mg. is sufficient for general well-being.

EXCESS/LACK
- Excess can cause a feeling of overstimulation, irritability, headaches or inability to sleep.
- High doses in women can cause facial hair, acne and/or deepening of the voice. This will cease when DHEA dose is reduced or discontinued.

TOXICITY ISSUES
- Do not take DHEA if you have an enlarged prostate or prostate cancer.

DOCTOR'S COMMENTS
- Although DHEA appears to be safe at low doses, many people take high doses to achieve a more pronounced effect. I do not advise this.
- If you are under the age of forty, your body is probably making all the DHEA you need. If you are over forty, you should have your DHEA levels checked to see if you are really deficient.
- There are some products available that are made from a plant of the Dioscorea family (wild yams found in abundance in Mexico) and are said to be DHEA

precursors or "natural" DHEA. These are not the same as pharmaceutical-grade DHEA and are virtually free of side effects.

DMAE
(2-DIMETHYLAMINOETHANOL)

NUTRIENT INFORMATION

- DMAE promotes the production of acetylcholine, which is the major neurotransmitter for memory and thought.
- This supplement is able to cross the blood-brain barrier and go immediately to the brain cells.
- It works best when combined with phosphatidyl choline and vitamin B5.

BENEFITS FOR YOUR BODY

- Enhances memory, especially short-term memory
- Increases mental function and concentration
- May be a natural alternative to Ritalin for children with ADD and hyperactivity
- May improve mood and sense of well-being
- Beneficial for Alzheimer's disease patients

BEST NATURAL SOURCES

- Seafood

HOW TO SUPPLEMENT

- Usual dose: 50–100 mg. daily
- Best if taken in the morning as it may cause central nervous system stimulation

EXCESS/LACK
- Too much may cause a feeling of excitability. If this happens cut back on the dosage.

TOXICITY ISSUES
- None reported

DOCTOR'S COMMENTS
- Some patients who take DMAE report improvement in memory and concentration in less than two weeks.
- CAUTION: Patients with epilepsy should not use DMAE as it may adversely affect this condition.

Dong Quai

NUTRIENT INFORMATION
- In Asia, dong quai is considered a woman's "tonic."
- It contains natural plant (phyto) estrogens.
- It is rich in vitamins A, B12 and E.
- Dong quai has diuretic properties as well, which means it helps body eliminate excess fluid.

BENEFITS FOR YOUR BODY
- Decreases hot flashes and night sweats
- Relieves PMS symptoms
- May prevent anemia
- Helps regulate menstrual periods
- Diminishes menstrual cramping

BEST NATURAL SOURCES
- Natural herb

HOW TO SUPPLEMENT
- Usual dose: 500 mg. twice daily

TOXICITY ISSUES
- None known

DOCTOR'S COMMENTS
- I usually do not prescribe dong quai separately. I prefer to recommend a good woman's formula that combines dong quai with other herbs.
- Do not use dong quai if you already have a heavy menstrual flow.
- Do not use during pregnancy as it relaxes the uterus and can cause miscarriage.
- It may cause some increased sensitivity to sunlight.

Echinacea

NUTRIENT INFORMATION
- Echinacea is one of the most highly regarded and potent immune support herbs available.
- It helps the body maintain its defense against viruses and bacteria.
- It stimulates growth of lymphocytes and macrophages (infection fighters).

BENEFITS FOR YOUR BODY
- Effective treatment against colds and flu
- Boosts immune system
- Effective in upper respiratory infections, including bronchitis

- Helps restore immune system after chemotherapy
- Helps fight candida albicans
- Effective in treatment of urinary tract infections and vaginal infections
- May help with treatment of herpes simplex virus
- May be helpful for tinnitus (ringing in ears)

BEST NATURAL SOURCES
- Natural herb

HOW TO SUPPLEMENT
- Usual dose: 500–1,000 mg. daily
- Often found in combination with goldenseal, another powerful immune-enhancer

EXCESS/LACK
- Excessive use will cause a decrease in effectiveness.

TOXICITY ISSUES
- Because this is a supplement that stimulates the immune system, people with autoimmune disorders should not use it.
- Do not use if you are allergic to sunflowers, marigolds or daisies (plants related to echinacea).

DOCTOR'S COMMENTS
- Echinacea is an herb that should not be used continuously, but should be cycled.
- I suggest you began echinacea at the first signs of an infection and continue through the course of the illness (eight to fourteen days).
- You may also take it preventatively throughout the flu season. Take daily for two weeks, and then take one week off. Repeat as desired.

EFAs—Essential Fatty Acids

NUTRIENT INFORMATION

- Essential fatty acids are called essential because the body cannot manufacture them.
- EFAs help the body produce hormones.
- They help regulate cholesterol and help to thin the blood.
- EFAs also contain anti-inflammatory compounds that relieve arthritis and autoimmune diseases.
- They can block tumor formation.
- There are three types of essential fatty acids:
    - Omega-3: Alpha linoleic acid that protects against cancer viruses and fungus. It also protects the body against potent forms of estrogen. Sometimes Omega-3 acids are broken down into eicosapentaenoic acid (EPA) and docosahexanoic acid (DHA).
    - Omega-6: Gamma-linoleic acid acts as a precursor to prostaglandins, which are hormones necessary for important body processes. Optimal ratio of Omega-6 to Omega-3 is 5:1.
    - Omega-9: Oleic acid is found in olive oil.

BENEFITS FOR YOUR BODY

- Prevent and treat heart disease, arthritis, stroke (Omega-3)
- Lower cholesterol (Omega-3, 6)
- Relieve eczema, psoriasis
- May help halt progression of MS (Omega-3)
- Prevent and relieve angina
- Reduce high blood pressure (Omega-3, 6)

- Prevent and treat rheumatoid arthritis (Omega-6)
- Help prevent cancer
- Relieve asthma and allergy symptoms
- Treat and prevent autoimmune diseases, including lupus
- Relieve constipation
- Enhance immune system
- Relieve PMS symptoms like irritability, headaches, breast tenderness (Omega-6)
- Relieve symptoms of skin disorders
- Maintain healthy skin
- Has anti-tumor effect against breast and colon cancer (flax)
- Helps relieve depression (Omega-3)
- Enhance circulatory system

BEST NATURAL SOURCES

- Omega-3: Tuna, salmon, halibut, mackerel, snapper, sesame, flax, pumpkin (good for vegetarians)
- Omega-6: Nuts, seeds, avocados, grains, walnuts; also found in evening primrose oil and borage oil
- Omega-9: Olive oil

HOW TO SUPPLEMENT

- Recommended dose of EFAs: 600–1,200 mg. of fish oils daily
- 1–2 tablespoons flaxseed oil daily OR ¼ cup ground flaxseed daily OR 600–1,200 mg. organic flaxseed in capsule form
- Omega-6: 750–1,200 mg. daily
- Note: Heating or cooking with these oils will destroy the EFAs in them.

EXCESS/LACK

- Deficiency signs are dry skin, loss of hair and a cold body.

TOXICITY ISSUES

- None at recommended doses

DOCTOR'S COMMENTS

- Because supplementation of EFAs can get complicated, I like to recommend products that have already combined the required amounts for you. These are some very good products that have been designed not to leave you with a fishy aftertaste.

- Supplementation of EFAs is a must as most people are extremely deficient.

- Note: Keep oils sealed from air and refrigerated to prevent rancidity. It is OK to keep smaller bottles are room temperature.

Feverfew

NUTRIENT INFORMATION
- Feverfew is an herb that has been used since ancient times to provide relief from fever. Its analgesic (pain-relieving) properties also provide relief from pains of arthritis and migraine headaches.
- Much clinical research has been done on feverfew in England where it is used widely.
- It helps slow the dilation of blood vessels.
- Feverfew appears to inhibit inflammation in the body.

BENEFITS FOR YOUR BODY
- Effective in headache relief
- May help decrease the frequency and intensity of migraine headaches
- Helps relieve the pain of arthritis
- Helps relieve dysmenorrhea (painful menstruation)
- May help in treatment of allergies

BEST NATURAL SOURCES
- Natural herb

HOW TO SUPPLEMENT
- Usual dose is 25 mg. twice daily.
- If you are experiencing a migraine headache, you may need to increase the dose to 1–2 grams.

EXCESS/LACK
- Excess use can lead to dermatitis (skin inflammation) or gastrointestinal upset.

TOXICITY ISSUES
- Toxicity is rare; however, if you develop mouth sores, discontinue use.

Supplements

103

DOCTOR'S COMMENTS

- In 1985, the *British Medical Journal* reported a study that showed feverfew to be effective in the prevention of migraine headaches.[4]
- At the very least, feverfew has been shown to reduce the symptoms of a migraine, including nausea and vomiting.
- If you suffer from migraines, I strongly suggest you try this herb.
- There are some reports that feverfew can interact with some medications, specifically aspirin or Coumadin, and change their effectiveness, so I do not recommend combining them.

Ginkgo Biloba

NUTRIENT INFORMATION

- Ginkgo biloba, one of the most commonly prescribed drugs in Europe, is best known for its restorative effects on the brain.
- It helps increase blood flow to the brain and the heart.
- It helps prevent lipofuscin deposits from atrophied cells in the brain.
- Ginkgo biloba is rich in flavonoids, which are powerful antioxidants.
- It increases the brain's ability to utilize glucose and produce energy.

BENEFITS FOR YOUR BODY

- Improves memory and mental function, especially short-term memory.
- Improves blood flow, especially to extremities
- Helps prevent blood clots in the body by inhibiting platelet aggregation
- Effective as a mood elevator
- May improve tinnitus (ringing in ears)
- May improve headaches, including migraines
- May help erectile dysfunction caused by inadequate blood flow
- Beneficial in macular degeneration of eyes and diabetic retinopathy
- Helps prevent age spots caused by lipofucsin deposits
- Holds promise for treatment of Alzheimer's disease; may delay and possibly reverse mental deterioration
- Has had beneficial effects on asthma

BEST NATURAL SOURCES

- Natural herb

HOW TO SUPPLEMENT

- Usual dose: 60 mg. 2–4 times per day

EXCESS/LACK

- Excess may lead to stomach upset or allergic skin reaction.

TOXICITY

- None known
- May occasionally cause a slight headache, which usually disappears after a few days

Supplements

105

- I highly recommend gingko biloba as an antiaging supplement to promote brain health and longevity. Hundreds of studies have been performed proving its effectiveness.
- Remember, it will be some time before you see the results from taking gingko biloba. Many people start to notice its benefits in two to three weeks, but it may take up to three months to notice your improvement.
- When selecting gingko biloba, be sure the product is standardized to contain 24 percent of gingko flavone glycosides as the active ingredient.

Ginseng

NUTRIENT INFORMATION

- Ginseng belongs to the group of herbs known as adaptogens. Adaptogens work to help the body adapt to stress and change and return to a balanced state.
- It has the ability to help the body inhibit the overproduction of cortisol.
- Panax ginseng, also called Korean or Chinese ginseng, is the most widely used ginseng.
- Siberian ginseng is usually less potent than Panax. Panax contains ginsenosides (phytochemicals that act as adaptogens).
- Ginseng is available as a root, a powdered extract and a liquid extract, as well as in tablets and capsules.

Supplements

BENEFITS FOR YOUR BODY

- Supports and strengthen the adrenal glands
- Reduces negative effects of chronic stress on the body
- Boosts energy levels
- Improves mental stamina
- Improves mood
- Improves mental performance and cognitive function
- Boosts libido
- May positively affect erectile dysfunction
- Increases immune function
- Reduces symptoms of chronic fatigue syndrome (Siberian)
- Helps the body resist stress-related illnesses
- Recommended as an antiaging tonic by many naturopathic physicians
- May boost estrogen levels in women and therefore may be helpful for menopause symptoms related to low estrogen (Chinese ginseng)

BEST NATURAL SOURCES

- Ginseng root

HOW TO SUPPLEMENT

- Usual dose for Panax ginseng is 75–100 mg. daily.
- Usual dose for Siberian ginseng is 150–300 mg. daily.
- All ginseng should be cycled, meaning to use it for four weeks and discontinue for two weeks.
- Do not exceed recommended doses.

TOXICITY ISSUES

- Do not take ginseng if you have high blood pressure.
- Do not take Panax ginseng if you take heart medication.
- Ginseng may occasionally cause vaginal bleeding in postmenopausal women.

- Panax causes some people to feel jittery and unable to sleep. It may cause heart palpitations at high doses.

DOCTOR'S COMMENTS

- Siberian ginseng has very few reported side effects.
- Not all ginseng products on the market are of the same quality. Look for products with the following standardized extracts: Siberian, 0.8 percent Eleutherosides; Panax, 7 percent Ginsenosides
- Many patients with chronic fatigue syndrome have experienced an increase in energy and immune function after taking Siberian ginseng.

Glucosamine

NUTRIENT INFORMATION

- Glucosamine is made in the body from glucose and the amino acid glutamine.
- It is involved in the formation of bones, ligaments and tendons.
- Glucosamine stimulates the manufacture of connective tissue important to mobility.
- Levels of glucosamine are believed to decline with age.

BENEFITS FOR YOUR BODY

- Relieves and reverses symptoms of osteoarthritis and rheumatoid arthritis
- Stimulates the production of new cartilage
- Increases healing and repair of joints
- Diminishes pain of arthritis

- Assists in the repair of ligaments and tendons as often seen in sports injuries
- Works best in combination with chondroitin (page 90)

BEST NATURAL SOURCES
- Natural dietary supplement

HOW TO SUPPLEMENT
- Usual form is glucosamine sulfate.
- Usual dose is 500 mg. three times daily.
- If gastric distress occurs, take with meals.

TOXICITY ISSUES
- None known

DOCTOR'S COMMENTS
- Numerous studies have indicated that glucosamine may be even more effective in the treatment of osteoarthritis than some of the more common prescription drugs. The good news is that the longer you use it, the better the results.
- Unlike NSAIDs (nonsteroidal anti-inflammatory drugs), glucosamine does not merely relieve the pain and inflammation of arthritis; it also helps repair the damaged joints.
- I recommend using glucosamine sulfate, as this is the form I have seen used in most of the scientific studies. Glucosamine is also available as glucosamine HCL and N-acetyl-glucosamine.

Grape Seed Extract
(Pycnogenol)

 NUTRIENT INFORMATION

- Pycnogenol is actually a patented name for pine bark extract. However, the term *pycnogenol* is often used to refer to other flavonoids as well.
- Pycnogenol is a potent blend of bioflavonoids.
- It acts as a powerful antioxidant, fifty times stronger than vitamins C or E.
- It acts as a free-radical scavenger at the cellular level to protect the body, especially grape seed extract.
- It promotes formation of skin proteins.

 BENEFITS FOR YOUR BODY

- Helps boost the immune system
- Protects against cancer
- Fights allergies and inflammation by reducing histamine production
- Maintains healthy skin; helps restore elasticity and smoothness
- Helps treat heart disease by keeping arteries healthy; strengthens blood vessels and capillary walls; helps prevent atherosclerosis
- Promotes circulation and oxygenation of the blood
- Treats varicose veins by promoting healthy vessels; inhibits destruction of collagen
- Helps detoxification from pollutants of smoking and alcohol
- Helps with liver detoxification
- May help halt the progression of arthritis (inhibits destruction of cartilage)

- Protects brain from mental deterioration due to free radicals

BEST NATURAL SOURCES
- Seeded grapes, green tea

HOW TO SUPPLEMENT
- Usual dose is 150–300 mg. daily.

EXCESS/LACK
- Too much green tea may cause overstimulation. If so, switch to a "caffeine-free" brand.

TOXICITY ISSUES
- None known

DOCTOR'S COMMENTS
- Antioxidants are one of the most powerful antiaging tools we have.
- Everyone should be on an antioxidant regimen, and the pycnogenols are an excellent choice.
- Remember, the next time you eat grapes, don't spit out the seeds!

Green Tea

NUTRIENT INFORMATION

- Green tea contains phytochemicals (catechins) that have been found to fight cancer and heart disease.
- It is rich in flavonoids, which are powerful antioxidants.
- Green tea is used heavily in Japan, which has one of the lowest rates of heart disease in the world.
- It contains a compound that has antibacterial properties.
- It also contains polyphenols that inhibit LDL ("bad") cholesterol.

BENEFITS FOR YOUR BODY

- Protects against cancer, especially lung, stomach and skin cancer
- Lowers cholesterol
- Promotes dental health and may decrease the number of cavities
- Helps prevent stroke; contains bioflavonoids that may help lower blood pressure
- May help with weight loss by increasing fat metabolism

BEST NATURAL SOURCES

- Natural herb

HOW TO SUPPLEMENT

- Drink three or more cups per day; five cups a day is preferred dose.
- It is also available in tablets that do not contain caffeine.

EXCESS/LACK

- Too much may cause overstimulation. If so, switch to a "caffeine-free" brand.

TOXICITY ISSUES

- None known

DOCTOR'S COMMENTS

- It may take several cups of brewed tea to get used to the taste, but it is actually very soothing in addition to all of its protective benefits.
- Some studies have suggested that green tea is as powerful an antioxidant as vitamin E.
- Green tea does contain caffeine in small amounts (20–30 mg. per cup), but it is much less than coffee, which contains about 100 mg. per 8-ounce cup.
- Black tea gives some of the same benefits but is not as protective overall. So think green!

Gugulipid

NUTRIENT INFORMATION

- Gugulipid is derived from the oleoresin extract of the Commiphora mukul tree of India.
- It contains steroid-like compounds that have cholesterol-lowering properties.

BENEFITS FOR YOUR BODY

- Lowers blood cholesterol
- Lowers blood triglycerides
- Raises HDL ("good") cholesterol
- Promotes cardiovascular health
- Helps prevent atherosclerosis

BEST NATURAL SOURCES

- Dietary supplement

HOW TO SUPPLEMENT

- Usual dose is 25 mg. three times a day.

TOXICITY ISSUES

- There are no known toxicity issues.
- Gugulipid does not have the side effects such as upset stomach and nausea that prescription lipid-lowering drugs do.

DOCTOR'S COMMENTS

- Gugulipid is found in many "healthy heart" formulas.
- Studies have indicated that it can lower cholesterol and triglycerides up to 25 percent in a four-week period.

Hawthorn

 NUTRIENT INFORMATION

- Hawthorn is an herb that has a concentrated source of flavonoids, which are powerful antioxidants and help strengthen capillaries.
- Hawthorn is well-researched and prescribed in Europe for people with heart problems.

 BENEFITS FOR YOUR BODY

- Helps lower cholesterol
- Improves blood supply to the heart by dilating the coronary blood vessels
- Reduces plaque in arteries
- Helps restore heart muscle and strengthens its ability to pump blood
- Helps reduce angina attacks
- Helps treat congestive heart failure
- Helps lower blood pressure

 BEST NATURAL SOURCES

- Natural herb

 HOW TO SUPPLEMENT

- Usual dose is 100–600 mg. daily.

 TOXICITY ISSUES

- None known

 DOCTOR'S COMMENTS

- It may take up to six weeks to notice the benefits of using hawthorn.

Supplements

IP6

NUTRIENT INFORMATION

- Inositol hexaphosphate, also known as phytic acid, is a component of fiber found in whole grains and beans.
- It regulates vital cell functions and protects cells from damage.
- IP6 boosts the body's natural resistance to disease.
- It has antitumor function.
- IP6 is a natural antioxidant; it binds to iron and prevents it from oxidizing.
- It is believed to inhibit division of cancer cells.[5]

BENEFITS FOR YOUR BODY

- Has powerful cancer-fighting properties
- Reduces risk of breast, colon and prostate cancer
- Boosts the immune system cells called "NK" (natural killer) cells, which can kill cancer cells and viruses
- Treats and prevents recurrence of kidney stones
- Prevents blood clots
- Lowers cholesterol and triglycerides

BEST NATURAL SOURCES

- Legumes (peas, beans), soybeans, corn, sesame seeds, wheat, cereals like rice and bran

HOW TO SUPPLEMENT

- Recommended dose is 800–1,200 mg. daily, taken on an empty stomach.
- If cancer is present, higher doses up to 6,000 mg. may be warranted.

TOXICITY ISSUES

- None reported, even at the higher doses

DOCTOR'S COMMENTS

- According to researchers, IP6 can be used beneficially in conjunction with ongoing chemotherapy and radiation treatments.
- Experimental studies from current research have shown IP6 to have the ability to shrink preexisting tumors and inhibit the growth of cancer. This may be one of science's most exciting new, natural tool against cancer.[6]

Isoflavones

NUTRIENT INFORMATION

- Isoflavones are a family of phytochemicals found in soy products that include the phytoestrogens, genistein and daidzein.
- It is found also in red clover, which provides all four of the estrogenic isoflavones: genistein, daidzein, biochanin and formononetin. (Please see page 141 for more important information on red clover.)
- They are powerful antioxidants that destroy free radicals.
- Isoflavones have mild estrogen-like activity and reduce effects of stronger estrogens on breast and endometrial tissue.
- They also balance the effect of testosterone on cells.

BENEFITS FOR YOUR BODY

- Lower cholesterol and triglyceride levels
- Reduce risk of heart disease by reducing plaque build-up in artery walls

117

- For menopause: relieve hot flashes; help vaginal dryness by stimulating growth of cells that line the vagina
- Powerful cancer fighters; inhibit cancer cell growth and reduce risk of lung, colon and stomach cancer
- Reduce risk of breast and endometrial cancer
- Inhibit growth of prostate cancer
- Help naturally balance estrogen levels

BEST NATURAL SOURCES
- Soy beans, soy milk, tofu, miso

HOW TO SUPPLEMENT
- Usual dose is 50–100 mg. daily.
- One-half cup of soybeans equals about 150 mg. of isoflavones

EXCESS/LACK
- Because our diets do not contain as many seeds, nuts, grains and beans as our ancestors' diets, most of us are probably deficient in the hormone-regulating substances known as isoflavones.

TOXICITY ISSUES
- CAUTION: If you have an existing breast malignancy, discuss any use of isoflavones with your doctor due to the fact that they do have phytoestrogenic properties.

DOCTOR'S COMMENTS
- Even though isoflavones have estrogenic properties, they function similar to antiestrogens when compared to estradiol. (Estradiol is a crystalline steroid produced by the ovary and possessing estrogenic properties.[7]) That is, they mimic estrogen and bind to the estrogen receptors in your body. This causes your body to make less of the more powerful estrogens and also prevents environmental xenoestrogens from occupying those receptor sites. In this way, they protect from the harmful effects of estradiol and estrone.

Supplements

- Many studies have been published showing that isoflavones are associated with a lower risk of breast cancer. With breast cancer occurring at alarmingly high rates in American women, the protection offered by isoflavones is very important to your health.

Kava

NUTRIENT INFORMATION

- Kava is an herb derived from the root of a tree that grows in islands of the Pacific.
- Its active ingredient is kava lactone.
- It promotes physical and mental relaxation.
- Unlike prescription drugs, it does not numb the mind.

BENEFITS FOR YOUR BODY

- Reduces anxiety
- Combats stress
- Induces feeling of alert calm followed by a feeling of sedation
- Promotes a sense of well-being
- Relaxes skeletal muscles
- Reduces depression
- Helpful for insomnia
- Soothes pain of urinary tract infections

BEST NATURAL SOURCES

- Natural herb

HOW TO SUPPLEMENT

- Usual dose is 150–600 mg. daily.
- Take for up to three months, and then discontinue for three to four weeks before starting again.
- Do not exceed recommended doses.

EXCESS/LACK

- High doses can cause a dry, scaly rash.
- Kava can cause allergic reactions and gastrointestinal discomfort in some people.

TOXICITY ISSUES

- Extremely high doses can cause paralysis.
- CAUTION: The Food and Drug Administration (FDA) is investigating the possibility that use of kava may cause liver toxicity. It urges consumers to watch for signs of liver trouble such as jaundice and brown urine, and to consult a physician if they experience less specific symptoms such as nausea, weakness and unusual tiredness.[8]

DOCTOR'S COMMENTS

- Use kava at the recommended doses only. This supplement should be used in cycles in order to give the body a rest from its effects.
- Remember, *do not* to stop taking any other antidepressant medication without the advice of your doctor.
- Do not drive while taking kava; it may cause drowsiness.
- It also can increase the effects of alcohol and other psychiatric drugs, so do not combine their use.

Lecithin

NUTRIENT INFORMATION

- Lecithin is a lipid that is needed by all cells in the body. It is a vital part of cell membranes, which control movement of nutrients on a cellular level throughout the body.
- It enables fats to be partially dissolved in water and removed from the body, protecting the heart and other vital organs from fatty buildup.

BENEFITS FOR YOUR BODY

- Controls cholesterol buildup in the organs and arteries
- Prevents arteriosclerosis and heart disease
- Prevents gallstones
- Helps repair alcohol damage to the liver
- Helps memory loss and "foggy brain" by keeping brain cell membranes healthy

BEST NATURAL SOURCES

- Soybeans, egg yolks, brewer's yeast, wheat germ

HOW TO SUPPLEMENT

- Usual dose: 1–2 Tbsp. granules daily
- Capsules: 1,200 mg. one to three times daily, before meals

EXCESS/LACK

- If we are deficient in lecithin, our body cannot make the proper amount of HDL ("good cholesterol").

TOXICITY ISSUES

- High doses can cause nausea, diarrhea and other gastrointestinal discomfort.

- Because so many people have eliminated egg yolks from their diets, they are not getting enough lecithin naturally.
- Lecithin is a relatively inexpensive supplement to add to your daily regimen. It is be especially beneficial to people over fifty to help with cardiovascular health.
- The powder form is very convenient to sprinkle on cereal or stir into soups, juice, water or a protein drink.

Licorice Root

NUTRIENT INFORMATION

- Licorice root contains glycyrrhizin, which may help balance hormone levels in women.
- It has strong antiviral properties as well as natural anti-inflammatory and antiallergic properties.
- Licorice root contains triterpenoids, which are being studied as powerful cancer-fighters by the Natural Cancer Institute.[9]
- Licorice root is also a good expectorant.

BENEFITS FOR YOUR BODY

- Relieves hot flashes
- Relieves PMS symptoms
- Has a positive effect on adrenal function; helps reverse adrenal exhaustion
- May prevent atherosclerosis (hardening of the arteries)
- Enhances immune system
- May be helpful in treatment of lupus
- May block tumor growth

Supplements

- Helpful for swelling and pain of arthritis
- Helps soothe discomfort of ulcers
- Good for sore throats and coughs
- Helps inhibit growth of the herpes simplex virus
- May help chronic fatigue syndrome symptoms

BEST NATURAL SOURCES
- Natural herb

HOW TO SUPPLEMENT
- Use as directed. It is often found in women's menopausal and PMS supplements in combination with other herbs.

EXCESS/LACK
- Excess use of licorice root may also promote water retention in some people, so it is not advised for anyone with a kidney disorder.

TOXICITY ISSUES
- CAUTION: People with high blood pressure should not use licorice root because it stimulates the body to produce aldosterone, a mineralocortiocoid hormone secreted by the adrenal cortex, which raises blood pressure.[10]
- Also, do not use licorice root if you have a history of glaucoma or stroke.

DOCTOR'S COMMENTS
- Candy licorice does not have the same medical benefits as products derived from the licorice root. However, in candy form, licorice can still cause an elevation in blood pressure.
- There is another form of licorice called DGL (deglycyrrhizinated licorice), which does not contain glycyrrhetinic acid and will not raise blood pressure. It enhances the protective mucus lining of the stomach and is a powerful antiulcer and gastritis treatment.

Supplements

Lutein

NUTRIENT INFORMATION

- Lutein is a carotenoid found in some green vegetables.
- The supplements are derived from marigold flower petals.
- Lutein helps protect the macula of the eye from the harmful effects of sunlight.
- It works as a powerful antioxidant that protects our vision.

BENEFITS FOR YOUR BODY

- Slows progression of retinitis pigmentosa (eye disease)
- Helps treat and prevent cataracts
- Helps prevent macular degeneration

BEST NATURAL SOURCES

- Kale, spinach, broccoli, mustard greens, Brussels sprouts, corn

HOW TO SUPPLEMENT

- Usual dose is 6–10 mg. per day.

TOXICITY ISSUES

- None known

DOCTOR'S COMMENTS

- Studies show that people who consume at least 6 mg. of lutein daily have a much lower incidence of macular degeneration of the eyes. Because it is difficult to get 6 mg. from our diet, I strongly recommend supplementation, especially for those with the highest risk for macular degeneration: people with blue, hazel or green eyes, postmenopausal women and anyone who smokes.

- I like to recommend a good eye vitamin formula that contains both lutein and bilberry along with zinc and vitamin C. Please begin to take it even if you are not having any vision problems!
- For all of us, lutein can prevent blindness and keeps our eyes strong and our vision clear.

Melatonin

NUTRIENT INFORMATION

- Melatonin is a hormone secreted by the pineal gland within the brain.
- Its levels peak at night and fall during the day, creating the body's sleep/wake cycle.
- Melatonin is best known for its role in promoting sleep, although some studies have shown that it may also slow the effects of aging.
- It plays an important role in immune function by activating cancer-fighting cells.
- The level of melatonin in the body decreases with age.

BENEFITS FOR YOUR BODY

- Aids in promoting sleep
- Boosts immune system, especially against cancer
- Useful in treatment of jet lag
- Helps counteract the damaging effects of stress by blocking the negative actions of corticosteroids
- May help protect against degenerative conditions of the brain as in Parkinson's and Alzheimer's disease
- May enhance libido by regulating sex hormones

- May enhance sexual pleasure by increasing the effect of endorphins, which often declines with age
- May have antiaging benefits according to recent studies

BEST NATURAL SOURCES
- Dietary supplement

HOW TO SUPPLEMENT
- Usual dose is .05–3 mg. taken at night.
- Oral: Take one and one-half hours before bedtime.
- Sublingual: Take one-half hour before bedtime.
- For jet lag, take one-half hour before you want to sleep.
- For people over age sixty-five, dose can be increased to 3–5 mg. taken at night.

EXCESS/LACK
- Low melatonin levels can lead to sleeping difficulties (abnormal sleep patterns).

TOXICITY ISSUES
- High doses may cause headaches, depression, vivid dreams and/or nightmares.
- Note: If the dose you take leaves you feeling groggy in the morning, it is too high and should be reduced.

DOCTOR'S COMMENTS
- Do not take melatonin if you are already taking tranquilizers.
- There is some concern that taking melatonin over a long term may have some negative side effects, although I have not seen any hard-core data. Because it is a hormone, it is wise to be cautious when supplementing melatonin. Occasional use is my preference.
- CAUTION: Do not drive after taking melatonin.

Milk Thistle

 NUTRIENT INFORMATION

- Milk thistle is an antioxidant, anti-inflammatory herb containing bioflavonoids.
- The active agent of milk thistle is silymarin, which acts as a powerful antioxidant for the liver.
- It stimulates growth of new liver cells.

 BENEFITS FOR YOUR BODY

- Cleanses the liver; enhances function
- Helps prevent cirrhosis, hepatitis, gallbladder disease
- Helps repair damaged or injured liver cells
- Helps detoxify liver from chemicals and pollutants
- May be beneficial for psoriasis, which is exacerbated by decreased liver function

 BEST NATURAL SOURCES

- Milk thistle is an herb whose fruit is an abundant source of silymarin.

 HOW TO SUPPLEMENT

- Usual dose is 320–350 mg. daily.

 TOXICITY ISSUES

- None known

 DOCTOR'S COMMENTS

- Almost everyone over the age of fifty should take milk thistle periodically as a supplement because our livers are so overtaxed by pollutants and toxins.
- You should especially take milk thistle if you drink, smoke or take prescription painkillers.
- A healthy liver can also better process excess estrogen in the body, which, as you know, can lead to many serious problems.

MSM

(Methylsulfonylmethane)

NUTRIENT INFORMATION

- MSM is a natural (organic) form of sulfur.
- Sulfur is essential to all cells in the body.
- It is vital to the production of amino acids.
- MSM is used by the body to build cartilage and collagen.
- It blocks pain impulses from traveling along nerve fibers.
- MSM plays a role in carbohydrate metabolism and insulin production.

BENEFITS FOR YOUR BODY

- Reduces pain and inflammation
- Increases blood flow to damaged tissues
- Helps reduce symptoms of arthritis, muscle pain, tendonitis, bursitis and carpal tunnel syndrome
- Helps relieve TMJ
- Helps reduce scar tissue
- May improve age-related hearing loss by increasing the elasticity of the tympanic membrane
- May help improve macular degeneration
- Promotes healthy hair and youthful skin
- May help diabetics metabolize carbohydrates properly

BEST NATURAL SOURCES

- Meats, eggs, poultry, dairy foods

HOW TO SUPPLEMENT

- Usual dose: 400–1000 mg. daily
- May be increased to 2,000–3,000 mg. daily for relief of arthritis pain

128

EXCESS/LACK
- High doses may cause some gastrointestinal discomfort.

TOXICITY ISSUES
- None known

DOCTOR'S COMMENTS
- MSM is organic sulfur and is nonallergenic. Do not confuse it with inorganic or synthetic sulfur, which can trigger allergic reactions in many people.
- For arthritis, MSM works well in combination with glucosamine to reduce pain and stiffness.

Supplements

129

NADH

(Nicotinamide Adenine Dinucleotide)

NUTRIENT INFORMATION

- NADH acts as an antioxidant that may help alleviate symptoms of Alzheimer's and Parkinson's disease.
- Also known as Coenzyme 1, NADH works with enzymes to produce chemical changes in the body.
- As a derivative of niacin, it helps cells produce energy.
- It is believed to raise dopamine levels (natural antidepressant).

BENEFITS FOR YOUR BODY

- May help improve symptoms of Parkinson's disease and Alzheimer's disease
- Protects against brain aging and deterioration
- May help boost libido and energy

BEST NATURAL SOURCES

- Dietary supplement

HOW TO SUPPLEMENT

- Usual dose is 2.5–5 mg. once or twice daily, taken one-half hour before eating.

EXCESS/LACK

- Low levels of NADH may contribute to depression and chronic fatigue as well as Alzheimer's disease.

TOXICITY ISSUES

- Rare

DOCTOR'S COMMENTS

- NADH is one of the lesser-known antioxidants, but it has been coming to the forefront lately due to studies that have linked supplementation of NADH with improvement in symptoms of Parkinson's and Alzheimer's diseases. If you have a loved one who suffers from either of these diseases, you should ask his physician about a trial usage of NADH.

Natural Progesterone

NUTRIENT INFORMATION

- In 1936, Japanese scientists used an extraction process and discovered dioscorea from the wild Mexican yam plant. It was found that the chemical configuration was almost identical to the progesterone excreted by the female ovaries. The United States Pharmacopoeia then standardized this to the form we know today as natural progesterone or USP progesterone.
- Progesterone levels decline to almost zero as a woman approaches or enters menopause due to anovulatory cycles. This fact runs contrary to the belief that a woman's estrogen levels decline to zero, which is a myth.
- Progesterone is the natural balance to estrogen in the body and is also necessary for the body's optimum use of estrogen.

BENEFITS FOR YOUR BODY

- There are numerous reports from millions of menopausal women who have stated that natural progesterone relieves their hot flashes, night sweats, insomnia, vaginal dryness, forgetfulness and fuzzy thinking.

- It helps relieve PMS symptoms of anxiety, irritability, mood swings, swollen breasts, depression, cramping and food cravings.
- It helps increase libido.
- It can alleviate depression.
- It helps relieve and reduce fibrocystic breasts.
- It helps build new bone.
- It may reduce size of fibroid tumors.
- It helps support thyroid function.
- It reduces simple ovarian cysts.
- Research shows that progesterone plays an important role in the health of the heart, brain and nerves as well.

BEST NATURAL SOURCES

- A natural supplement made from sterols extracted from wild yams and converted to progesterone in the laboratory

HOW TO SUPPLEMENT

- Look for a transdermal cream that contains at least 960 mg. of micronized USP progesterone per 2-ounce jar or tube.
- Usual dose is ¼ tsp. (creams) two times daily.
- Menopausal women use it daily for twenty-six days of the month.
- Women with PMS or who are still menstruating and using it for libido, breast disease and so on, use it from day 12 thru 26 of each menstrual cycle.
- It is also available in oral form.

TOXICITY ISSUES

- There are no known toxicity issues.
- It is even safe for women with a history of miscarriage to use during pregnancy.
- Unlike synthetic progestins, USP progesterone has 0 percent risk of breast cancer, stroke, heart attack and blood clots.

DOCTOR'S COMMENTS

- All women suffering from PMS or experiencing peri-menopause and menopause should use progesterone cream in order to balance hormone levels.
- It is excellent treatment for osteoporosis as it helps build new bone. Clinical studies have shown that some women had a 10–15 percent increase in bone density after using natural progesterone.
- Recent studies have shown that natural progesterone is especially protective against breast cancer as well as other reproductive organ cancers. Studies indicate that women diagnosed with breast cancer who had high progesterone levels had better survival rates.
- Due to the increasing number of studies showing the multiple roles of this remarkable hormone, I predict that natural progesterone will be in every American medicine cabinet by the year 2015, just as aspirin is in every medicine cabinet today.
- Dr. John R. Lee highly recommends it for men with enlarged prostates.
- Note: You may find more information on natural progesterone and its uses or recommendations of a reputable product by visiting my website at www.askdrhelen.com.

Olive Leaf Extract

NUTRIENT INFORMATION
- Olive leaf extract contains elenolic acid, which has been found to have antibacterial and antiviral properties.
- It is able to stop bacteria and viruses from multiplying.
- It also has antifungal properties.

BENEFITS FOR YOUR BODY
- Helps naturally lower blood pressure; increases blood flow in coronary system
- Prevents oxidation of LDL ("bad") cholesterol
- Acts like a natural antibiotic to fight against colds and viruses
- Effective against parasitic infections
- Useful for treatment of fungal infections
- May be helpful in treating candida albicans (yeast infections)
- Effective against herpes viruses
- Reduces tiredness and fatigue and increases energy
- Has also been used to treat Epstein-Barr and mononucleosis

BEST NATURAL SOURCES
- Extract

HOW TO SUPPLEMENT
- Usual dose: 500 mg. once or twice a day for colds, flu or infections
- For chronic fatigue, may increase dose to 500 mg. three times daily

TOXICITY ISSUES

- Has been found to be extremely nontoxic even at high doses

DOCTOR'S COMMENTS

- Olive leaf extract is one of my favorite supplements.
- Remember, using olive leaf extract creates dead microbes, which release toxins. As your body is working to eliminate these, you may experience a period of minimal discomfort including headaches or joint pain. This is called the "die-off" effect. It rarely lasts more than four days. During this time, drink lots of water to help flush the kidneys and look forward to feeling great!

Oregano Oil

NUTRIENT INFORMATION

- Oregano oil contains fifty powerful healing compounds.
- The most active compound in oregano oil is carvacrol, a natural antimicrobe agent.
- It has antiseptic properties.
- Oregano oil also contains antioxidant and immune-enhancing compounds.

BENEFITS FOR YOUR BODY

- Treats fungal infections
- Fights colds and flu
- Fights and protects against bacterial infections
- Relieves pain of arthritis, strains, sprains and nerve pain

- Treats parasite infections
- May help stop onset of migraine headaches
- Relieves eczema and psoriasis
- Treats cold and canker sores
- Relieves allergies, asthma, bronchitis and sinusitis
- Treats warts and toe fungus

BEST NATURAL SOURCES
- Essential oil derived from the oregano plant

HOW TO SUPPLEMENT
- Capsules: 1–2 daily
- Liquid: 1–2 drops in 4 oz. of water or juice once or twice per day
- Safe for children if you use one-half of adult dose

TOXICITY ISSUES
- Do not take internally for a period exceeding twenty-one days, or it may negatively affect liver function.

DOCTOR'S COMMENTS
- Please be sure your product contains Origanum vulgare, which is true oregano.
- Many forms of oregano are actually made from thyme or marjoram and do not contain the same healing components.

Phosphatidylserine (PS)

 NUTRIENT INFORMATION
- PS is a phospholipid (fat) that helps support the brain and its function.
- It helps relay messages between the cells of the brain.
- PS helps the brain retrieve information.
- Levels of PS in the body decline with age.

 BENEFITS FOR YOUR BODY
- Studies show PS improves memory loss due to aging.
- It improves concentration and cognitive function.
- It may have some effect on senility and Alzheimer's disease.
- It may inhibit elevation of cortisol levels due to stress, reducing harmful effects on the body.
- It improves mood.

 BEST NATURAL SOURCES
- Dietary supplement

 HOW TO SUPPLEMENT
- Usual dose is 100 mg. twice daily for one month. Then, for maintenance, take 100 mg. once a day.

 TOXICITY ISSUES
- None known

 DOCTOR'S COMMENTS
- PS is considered by many physicians who prescribe antiaging techniques to be the most effective brain nutrient available at this time.

- PS is not cheap, but it is valuable because it may have the ability to restore the brain to its maximum activity.
- As with any brain nutrient, I strongly suggest that you purchase from a very reputable company.

Pregnenolone

NUTRIENT INFORMATION

- Pregnenolone is a hormone made primarily in the adrenal glands but also in the brain.
- It can be metabolized into progesterone.
- The levels of pregnenolone in our body decline with age.
- It was used widely as a natural treatment for arthritis before cortisone was discovered.

BENEFITS FOR YOUR BODY

- Improves and enhances memory
- Increases mental alertness, clarity of thought
- Enhances visual perception
- Elevates mood; called the "feel good" hormone
- Restores youthful vigor and vitality
- Increases resistance to stress
- Helps balance estrogen levels
- Has a positive effect on RA (rheumatoid arthritis) and lupus
- Has a positive effect on cholesterol

BEST NATURAL SOURCES
- Dietary supplement

HOW TO SUPPLEMENT
- Usual dose is 5–10 mg. per day.
- It is also available as a sublingual tablet.

EXCESS/LACK
- Some people report that too much pregnenolone causes a feeling of overstimulation or nervousness.

TOXICITY ISSUES
- None known with proper doses

DOCTOR'S COMMENTS
- Just 5 mg. daily can do much to help balance hormones and improve mood. If you have never taken it before, you may want to start by using it once or twice a week only.
- Pregnenolone is one of the supplements I use most successfully to treat depression that often accompanies menopause.
- CAUTION: Do not use pregnenolone if you are at risk for hormonally related cancers such as reproductive or prostate cancer.

Pygeum

NUTRIENT INFORMATION

- Pygeum is an herb derived from the bark of an African tree.
- It is believed to interfere with enzymes that promote prostate cell growth and inflammation.
- Pygeum contains phytosterols, which have anti-inflammatory properties.
- It is a natural diuretic.

BENEFITS FOR YOUR BODY

- Prevents and reduces an enlarged prostate
- Reduces symptoms of BPH, including frequent night-time urination, painful urination and interrupted flow of urine
- Aids in treatment of urinary tract infections

BEST NATURAL SOURCES

- Natural herb

HOW TO SUPPLEMENT

- Usual dose: 100–200 mg. daily

TOXICITY ISSUES

- None known

DOCTOR'S COMMENTS

- Today there are many excellent men's formulas available that combine the natural substances known to reduce BPH. Some of these natural substances include saw palmetto, zinc, pygeum and stinging nettle.
- Finding a good men's prostate health formula can eliminate the need to take all of these supplements separately and usually increases compliance.

Red Clover

NUTRIENT INFORMATION

- Red clover is a phyto-estrogenic herb well studied for its support during menopause.
- It is a powerful source of isoflavones (contains genistein, biochanin, daidzein and formononetin) and has a balancing effect on estrogen levels. If levels are high, it occupies the receptor sites and blocks more powerful estrogens; if levels are low, it has a stimulating effect.
- It also contains choline, calcium and lecithin.
- Red clover is also a mild diuretic.

BENEFITS FOR YOUR BODY

- Diminishes hot flashes
- Has been found to contribute to breast health
- Protects against breast, colon and prostate cancer
- May help reduce symptoms of endometriosis
- Helps restore moisture to dry vulva and vaginal tissues
- Studies indicate it supports bone health
- Supports cardiovascular health
- Helps in treatment of eczema and psoriasis
- Has expectorant properties that help in treatment of asthma and bronchitis
- May help with bloating

BEST NATURAL SOURCES

- Dietary supplement

HOW TO SUPPLEMENT

- Usual dose: 40–100 mg. daily (capsules)
- Available as a transdermal creme blended with USP progesterone to be used ¼ tsp. twice daily for twenty-six days of the month

- Also available as a tincture: take 30 drops daily in warm water

TOXICITY ISSUES

- Human toxicity is rare.

DOCTOR'S COMMENTS

- I do not advise any woman to take red clover as a supplement without balancing it with natural progesterone, because it can lead to the symptoms of estrogen dominance, an unhealthy condition for the body.
- When balanced with USP progesterone, this herb has been found to relieve hot flashes, night sweats, insomnia, vaginal dryness, anxiety, depression, mood swings, forgetfulness, rapid skin aging and a loss of tone in breasts.
- My Menopause Relief Cream, based on red clover, also contains 1,000 mg. of USP progesterone.
- CAUTION: Due to its estrogenic activity, your physician may not want you to use red clover if you have an existing cancer, especially breast or prostate cancer. Natural progesterone would be a good choice instead.

SAM-e
(S-adenosylmethionine)

 NUTRIENT INFORMATION
- Made in the liver from the amino acid methionine
- May increase brain levels of dopamine and serotonin
- Used widely in Europe

 BENEFITS FOR YOUR BODY
- Has been found effective in treatment of depression
- May help reduce arthritis pain and suffering
- May help with fibromyalgia

 BEST NATURAL SOURCES
- Dietary supplement

 HOW TO SUPPLEMENT
- Usual dose is 400–800 mg. daily.

 TOXICITY ISSUES
- None known. It does not seem to cause adverse effects even at high doses.

 DOCTOR'S COMMENTS
- This nutrient is quite expensive.
- If you have tried St. John's Wort for depression and not found it effective, you may want to give SAM-e a trial.
- Remember NEVER to wean yourself off prescription antidepressants quickly or without your physician's knowledge.

Supplements

Saw Palmetto

NUTRIENT INFORMATION

- Saw palmetto is an herb that inhibits the production of dihydrotestosterone, which contributes to enlargement of the prostate.
- It is used extensively in Europe and is now being used in the United States to treat benign prostate hypertrophy.

BENEFITS FOR YOUR BODY

- Reduces prostate size, pain and blockage
- Increases urine flow and decreases nighttime urination in men with BPH
- Improves general prostate health
- May help stimulate the libido

HOW TO SUPPLEMENT

- Usual dose is 160 mg. twice daily.

TOXICITY ISSUES

- Some mild rare side effects may include headache or slight stomach upset.

DOCTOR'S COMMENTS

- Studies have shown that saw palmetto works just as well as the prescription drug Proscar in many cases of prostate enlargement, without the negative side effects of the drug therapy such as decreased libido, ejaculation problems and even impotence.
- Allow yourself four to six weeks to notice the improvement.
- I think all men over the age of fifty should take the supplement saw palmetto as a preventative measure.

Supplements

Serotonin

5-Hydroxytryptamine (5-HTP)

NUTRIENT INFORMATION
- Serotonin gives the body a feeling of contentment.
- 5-HTP helps the body increase its natural serotonin levels.
- It also controls sensitivity to pain and helps us sleep.
- Effects are similar to the amino acid L-tryptophan, which is available by prescription only.

BENEFITS FOR YOUR BODY
- May eliminate craving for carbohydrates
- A natural antidepressant
- Reduces stress
- Aids a good night's sleep
- Found to suppress appetite in some people

BEST NATURAL SOURCES
- Dietary supplement

HOW TO SUPPLEMENT
- Usual dose is 50–100 mg. daily.

EXCESS/LACK
- Low levels of serotonin can lead to depression, anxiety and overeating of carbohydrates.

TOXICITY ISSUES
- None known

DOCTOR'S COMMENTS
- 5-HTP has been used by many as an alternative to Prozac and has proven to be quite effective without any negative side effects.

- If you are considering switching to 5-HTP, please remember that you must wean off your other antidepressant medication. This should be done under the supervision of your physician.
- Do not combine 5-HTP with MAO inhibitor type medications.

St. John's Wort

NUTRIENT INFORMATION
- St. John's Wort is an herb used in centuries-old treatments and popular in Europe for depression, anxiety and gastric ulcers.
- It appears to alter brain chemistry as it applies to mood improvement.
- It may help increase brain's dopamine production.

BENEFITS FOR YOUR BODY
- A natural antidepressant, reportedly good for mild to moderate depression
- Greatly improves sleep quality
- Relieves insomnia
- May improve painful menses and uterine cramping

BEST NATURAL SOURCES
- Natural herb

HOW TO SUPPLEMENT
- 300 mg. two to three times daily

EXCESS/LACK
- Use of St. John's Wort may cause photosensitivity, so

avoid exposure to direct sunlight while using it.

TOXICITY ISSUES

- Possibly toxic with high doses, so use only recommended dosage

DOCTOR'S COMMENTS

- Research has shown that St. John's Wort may be more effective in relieving depression than prescription drugs without the undesirable side effects (such as reduction in sex drive and drug "hangover").

- Remember, if you are taking a prescription drug for depression, don't stop taking the prescription drug without your physician's supervision.

- CAUTION: A recent study indicates that St. John's Wort may decrease the effects of certain chemotherapy drugs in the treatment of cancer. If you are undergoing chemotherapy, you should not use St. John's Wort until further studies are performed to verify this data.[11]

Supplements

Tribulus Terrestris

 NUTRIENT INFORMATION
- Tribulus terrestris is an ancient herb long used in India and China to enhance sexual performance.
- It is believed to stimulate the production of testosterone by causing the pituitary to release luteinizing hormone (LH).
- It is used in Europe by bodybuilders, especially in Russia, and was imported to the United States.

 BENEFITS FOR YOUR BODY
- According to European medical literature, may increase sex drive
- May increase strength of erections and sperm production
- Builds lean muscle mass

 BEST NATURAL SOURCES
- Dietary supplement

 HOW TO SUPPLEMENT
- Usual dose is 650 mg. daily.

 TOXICITY ISSUES
- Avoid tribulus terrestris if you have any history of prostate problems.

 DOCTOR'S COMMENTS
- This herb is safe and relatively inexpensive.
- It may not produce results in everyone who takes it, but anecdotal reports so far are positive from both men and women.

Valerian Root

NUTRIENT INFORMATION
- Valerian root is an herbal tranquilizer and muscle relaxant.
- It binds to the GABA-A receptors in the brain that regulate sedation.
- Valerian root is used widely in Europe to treat anxiety.
- It is not habit-forming.
- Valerian root may be taken during the day to treat anxiety without drowsy side effects.

BENEFITS FOR YOUR BODY
- Helps with insomnia, especially if insomnia is a result of anxiety and nervousness
- A good treatment for anxiety and nervousness
- Helps reduce panic attacks
- Helps treat menstrual cramps
- Helps reduce muscle tension, spasms and muscle cramps
- May help with mood swings

BEST NATURAL SOURCES
- Natural herb

HOW TO SUPPLEMENT
- For insomnia: Usual dose is 150–300 mg. taken thirty to forty-five minutes before bedtime.

EXCESS/LACK
- Unknown

TOXICITY ISSUES
- Extremely high doses can be toxic and cause paralysis.

DOCTOR'S COMMENTS

- Patients who use valerian for insomnia have reported that they experienced no morning "hangover" or drowsy feeling.
- Valerian seems to work as well as prescription tranquilizers in many people without the negative side effects of prescription drugs.

Yohimbe

NUTRIENT INFORMATION

- Yohimbe is an herb derived from the bark of a tree found in West Africa.
- It is sold under the name of Yohimbe or Yohimbine HCL.
- Yohimbine HCL is sold by prescription only. Yohimbe is a weaker version available in health food stores.
- Studies have shown effectiveness in treatment of impotence. However, please be careful to heed cautions below.

BENEFITS FOR YOUR BODY

- Increases blood flow to penis; aids impotence
- Increases libido

HOW TO SUPPLEMENT

- Usual dose: 500 mg. once or twice a day

TOXICITY ISSUES

- Do not take if you have low blood pressure or heart problems or if you take antidepressant medication.
- Do not take if you have kidney disease.

DOCTOR'S COMMENTS

- WARNING: Yohimbe has very powerful side effects, including anxiety, hallucinations, elevated blood pressure or sudden drop in blood pressure, headache and dizziness.
- It is considered by the FDA to be unsafe.
- I do not recommend use of this herb. Instead, please try tribulus terrestris, avena sativa, gingko biloba or L-arginine.
- If you do take yohimbe, do so only under a physician's supervision.

Recommendations
for Common
Conditions

I consider it my privilege to bring to you the knowledge and expertise of the many health care experts I have interviewed over the years as host of the *Doctor to Doctor* television program, along with the latest updates in natural treatments available for each condition.

Please bear in mind that the natural substances listed may not include every supplement that can help a particular problem, but they serve as an overview of those treatments currently recognized and embraced by many leading experts.

After viewing the listed supplements for your condition, you can refer to each one that is highlighted in the previous sections of this reference guide for more helpful information about how to use them.

I would enjoy hearing from you readers who implement these suggested regimens and find they have truly helped restore you to optimum health.

Acne

RECOMMENDED SUPPLEMENTS

- Folic acid
- Zinc
- Vitamin B5 (antistress vitamin)

Doctor James E. Fulton, co-inventor of Retin-A and a board-certified dermatologist and plastic surgeon, shared with me that benzoyl peroxide is also one of the most powerful tools available for the treatment of acne. When applied daily, benzoyl peroxide diffuses into the skin and kills the bacteria deep in the pore. It also causes peeling and loosening of impactions on the surface of the skin. Dr. Fulton discovered this action when he was experimenting with benzoyl peroxide in 1970.[1]

In addition to taking the supplements listed, I recommend that you give benzoyl peroxide a try. When used as directed, my patients reported positive, healing results in both mild and severe cases of acne.

Allergies/Hayfever

- Vitamin B12
- Vitamin C
- Quercetin
- Gingko biloba
- EFAs, especially Omega-6
- Beta-glucan
- Pycnogenol
- Oregano oil
- Feverfew

In addition to the supplements listed, a study published in the *Lancet* involving 2,633 subjects indicated that vitamin E may be valuable in reducing the antibodies associated with asthma and allergies.[2] One more use for one of our favorite supplements, the powerful little vitamin E!

Alzheimer's Disease

RECOMMENDED SUPPLEMENTS
- Vitamin E
- Gingko biloba
- Phosphatidylserine
- L-carnitine
- Vitamin B complex, especially B12
- Folic acid
- Choline
- Melatonin
- DHEA
- Glutathione
- NADH

So many of the doctors and researchers I have interviewed over the years have told me that studies published in the *New England Journal of Medicine* and other well-established medical journals show that vitamin E can delay the onset of Alzheimer's disease among adults with early-onset brain aging.[3] I encourage everyone to take vitamin E as a supplement. It is one of the least expensive supplements on the market and easily one of the most important.

Anemia

RECOMMENDED SUPPLEMENTS
- Vitamin B complex
- Vitamin C
- Iron
- Dong quai

If you are anemic, you may suffer from a severe vitamin C deficiency, because it is vitamin C that helps the body absorb and use iron. My friend and colleague Bill Sardi, who has appeared many times on the *Doctor to Doctor* television program, has advised that the vitamin C you get from drinking orange juice or from taking a vitamin pill will increase your absorption of iron. He adds, however, that not all cases of anemia are caused by iron deficiency.[4]

In his book *The Iron Time Bomb,* Bill Sardi states that anemia may be one of the most over-diagnosed and overtreated disorders. He says that mild anemia may often just be the body's protective response to infection or disease.[5]

Vitamin B12 and folic acid deficiency can also cause anemia. The most common causes of iron-deficiency anemia are excessive menstrual blood loss, regular blood donation, intensive endurance training, chronic aspirin use and a strict vegetarian or macrobiotic diet.

You should never take an iron supplement without a blood test indicating that you are truly suffering from iron-deficiency anemia. Any treatment for anemia should focus on the underlying

157

causes for the chronic blood loss or other reason the individual is not absorbing sufficient amounts of dietary iron naturally.

Also, anemia among the very old (over eighty-five years of age) is a strong indication of disease and possibly blood loss somewhere in the body. It is very important for these precious elderly people to have regular exams that include blood work.

Angina

(see also Heart Disease)

 RECOMMENDED SUPPLEMENTS
- L-carnitine
- Hawthorn

 Angina pectoris is characterized by a squeezing or pressure-like pain in the chest that appears quickly after exertion. It may radiate to the shoulder blade, arm or even the jaw. Angina is caused by an insufficient supply of oxygen to the heart muscle and is usually a result of athero-sclerosis. It is a serious condition that requires strict medical supervision.

If you are having chest pain, whether you are male or female, please seek medical help immediately. Supplements are not meant to be a substitute for medical care in the treatment of angina or other cardiovascular ailments. Do not use them without alerting your physician.

Antiaging Supplements

RECOMMENDED SUPPLEMENTS

- Natural progesterone
- Pregnenolone
- DHEA
- Gingko biloba
- L-glutamine
- Phosphatidylserine (PS)
- L-carnitine
- DMAE
- Coenzyme Q-10
- Melatonin
- EFAs
- Grape seed extract (pycnogenol)
- Alpha lipoic acid
- Selenium
- Vitamin E
- Ginseng

I regularly attend many antiaging conventions, and I must tell you that I meet some of the most dedicated and fascinating physicians and researchers there. Many of them have been willing to share their important studies with my audience even before they have published them. I have compiled this list of supplements for you based on the latest research regarding the aging process.

As new discoveries are made and clinical testing

Recommendations

is done, I will continue to bring it to you on the *Doctor to Doctor* television program and also publish it on my website: www.askdrhelen.com.

Anxiety

RECOMMENDED SUPPLEMENTS

- Vitamin B complex
- Vitamin B6
- Vitamin B12
- St. John's Wort
- Calcium/magnesium
- 5-HTP
- Kava (Please refer to caution for this supplement.)
- Valerian root

You may be thinking, *Well, everybody has anxiety today*. That may be true for most people sporadically, but if you suffer from chronic anxiety, it can be so debilitating as to interfere with your living a normal life. What are the symptoms?

Dr. Ray Sahelian, director of the Longevity Research Institute in Marina del Ray, California, defines them for us as a chronic feeling of tenseness, inability to relax and focus, irritability, inability to sleep, elevated blood pressure, heart palpitations, gastrointestinal symptoms such as irritable bowel, upset stomach, indigestion, headaches, hives and hair-pulling.[6]

In addition to the supplements listed, Dr.

Sahelian suggests other ways to eliminate chronic anxiety are to get away from your immediate environment by taking a one-day vacation or a long weekend, join an exercise class and PRAY! (Yes, prayer has been clinically proven to alleviate anxiety!)

Arthritis

RECOMMENDED SUPPLEMENTS

- Glucosamine
- Chondroitin
- Beta carotene
- Vitamins A and C
- Vitamin B complex
- Vitamin E
- SAM-e
- MSM
- EFAs
- Pycnogenol
- Feverfew

One of my favorite stories about the effectiveness of the ministry of Trinity Broadcasting Network that has brought the *Doctor to Doctor* television program to its viewers for the past eleven years relates directly to the subject of arthritis.

In 1990, Dr. Joseph Pizzorno, president and cofounder of Bastyr College, told our audience about the benefits of glucosamine in the treatment of arthritis. At the time, we did not even know what the substance was. Now, glucosamine can be found in most stores, and even hard-core, mainstream doctors not inclined to using natural supplements are recommending it for their arthritis patients.[7]

This testimonial goes to the heart of the matter, which is my strong conviction that God has provided many natural substances to use for our healing. And it is thrilling for me to see how these natural supplements are being recognized now through time-tested results for their wonderful healing properties.

Asthma

 RECOMMENDED SUPPLEMENTS

- Magnesium
- Vitamin B6
- Vitamin C
- EFAs, especially Omega-3
- Beta-glucan
- Alpha lipoic acid
- Coenzyme Q-10
- Oregano oil
- Bioflavonoids, especially quercetin
- Choline
- N-acetylcysteine (NAC)
- Gingko biloba

Dr. Joseph Pizzorno of Bastyr University told me that many studies have indicated that food allergies play an important role in asthma. Double-blind food studies in children have shown the worst offenders to be (in decreasing order): eggs, fish, shellfish, nuts and peanuts. Others that are problematic are milk, chocolate, wheat and citrus. Elimination diets have been successful in treating asthma in infants and children. He said it is also very important to eliminate food additives such as artificial dyes and preservatives.[8]

Dr. Stephen Levine, who holds a Ph.D. from the University of California, Berkeley, brought this exciting research to our audience: Studies based on the work of Dr. Buteyko, a Russian physician, showed that many asthmatics have a breathing problem that is similar to people who hyperventilate and that their carbon dioxide-oxygen ratio is different from that of a normal person. He told us that people who are having an asthma attack might benefit from breathing into a paper bag to thwart the asthmatic attack. This technique may cut down on the use of a steroid inhaler.[9]

Breast Cancer

RECOMMENDED SUPPLEMENTS

- Natural progesterone
- Vitamin E
- Vitamin C
- Selenium
- Isoflavones
- IP6
- Coenzyme Q-10
- EFAs, especially Omega-6

You may have heard me speaking out against the use of synthetic hormones (HRT and birth control pills) for many years. A study published in the *Journal of the American Medical Association* (February 2002) states that the incidence of breast cancer increased by 60 to 85 percent with long-term use of HRT, whether estrogen alone or estrogen plus progestin.[10] This statistic is appalling! It is even worse than the 46 percent increase I had been projecting for the past ten years.

The good news is that other studies have confirmed that natural progesterone is not only beneficial in helping to prevent breast cancer, but can actually work to contain it and increase a woman's chances of survival.[11] All of these studies, including one from Johns Hopkins University, indicating that progesterone protects against breast cancer are posted on my website: www.askdrhelen.com. I urge you to visit the site and download the studies. I believe that all women should have a jar of natural progesterone in their medicine cabinet and use it daily!

165

Cancer

RECOMMENDED SUPPLEMENTS

- Beta carotene
- Selenium
- Vitamin C
- Vitamin E
- B complex
- Coenzyme Q-10
- EFAs
- Beta-glucan
- Green tea
- Aloe vera
- IP6
- Isoflavones
- Pycnogenol

Several years ago, I interviewed Dr. Robert Atkins (known for his Atkins Diet). He told me that he believes that someday cancer may become a chronic condition, like diabetes, that a patient can tolerate rather than the life-threatening disease that cancer is now. He thinks that one day it may be unnecessary for cancer patients to risk surgery or chemotherapy and radiation, toxic modalities that can cause death.[12]

Burton Goldberg, editor of *Alternative Medicine* magazine, more recently told me that it is his conviction as well. He feels the ravaging effects of cancer can be reduced to the level of a chronic disease, which can be treated so that quality of life is not disrupted. I have great hope that we are moving in that direction.

Recommendations

We are certainly making great breakthroughs in the field of integrative medicine, which combines conventional therapies with naturopathic medicine for the cancer patient. I firmly believe that anyone who has cancer should take immune-boosting supplements to restore health to their bodies in addition to any other cancer therapies they are undergoing.

In addition to the supplements listed above, don't forget what I have been telling my viewers for many years—garlic helps fight cancer! That's right, it contains disulfides that are not only antifungal and antibacterial, but anticancer as well.

I would also like to remind you that Dr. Francisco Contreras, noted oncologist and director of the Oasis of Hope Hospital in Baja California, Mexico, stressed that we are not just physical beings, but spiritual and emotional beings as well. Belief in God and a positive attitude are vital tools in stimulating the immune system and facilitating healing.[13]

Recommendations

Candida Albicans

RECOMMENDED SUPPLEMENTS

- Acidophilus
- Echinacea
- Olive leaf extract

Experts have told me that our diet of excessive sugar and carbohydrates is largely responsible for the increase in cases of candida in our population. If you suffer from the symptoms of candida, you should eliminate the following foods from your diet altogether until symptoms subside: all breads containing gluten, aged cheeses, fermented foods, vinegar, wine, beer and chocolate. Only after returning to normalcy should you attempt to add these foods into your diet, and only then in moderation.

Oral contraceptives also contribute toward increased susceptibility. If you are interested in a vaginal gel I developed with Dr. Perry Ratcliff, which is extremely effective against candida, please visit my website for more information.

Chronic Fatigue Syndrome

RECOMMENDED SUPPLEMENTS

- Olive leaf extract
- Coenzyme Q-10
- Vitamin B complex
- Beta-glucan
- DHEA
- NADH
- Siberian ginseng
- Vitamin C
- Vitamin E
- Magnesium
- Licorice root

I had the great honor of interviewing Dr. Jeffrey S. Bland, president of HealthComm, Inc. of Gig Harbor, Washington. He told me that most chronic fatigue sufferers have a magnesium deficiency inside their cells. Thus the cells are unable to utilize nutrients and more likely to accumulate toxic by-products, thereby possibly reducing the cells' energy functions.

In the past, patients suffering from chronic fatigue were advised to get more rest, improve their nutrition and lead a healthier lifestyle. We now know that this is not the answer and can cause great frustration for people with CFS. There is constant research going on in this field. An excellent resource is the *Fibromyalgia Network,* a newsletter for people with fibromyalgia and chronic fatigue syndrome (P. O. Box 31750, Tucson, AZ 85751-1750; www.fmnetnews.com). The newsletter was begun in 1984 in an effort to bring you the latest developments in treatment as well as offer tips for everyday living with these painful conditions.

Circulation Problems

RECOMMENDED SUPPLEMENTS
- Gingko biloba
- EFAs
- Vitamin E
- Bioflavonoids
- Pycnogenol

One of the most interesting interviews I have conducted was with Dr. Alan Sosin, director of the Sand Canyon Medical Center in Irvine, California. He told me about a therapy called EECP (Enhanced External Counter Pulsation), which is a nonsurgical therapy that dramatically improves circulation by pumping blood from the legs to the heart. It increases circulation and expands the vessels in the heart. It causes blood to by-pass vessels that are blocked and increases circulation to the heart muscle. EECP works in synchronization with your own heart.

EECP therapy was approved by the FDA in 1995 for the treatment of angina and has been studied for the treatment of other circulatory disorders. It is usually given in a series of one-hour treatments. Dr. Sosin told us that Medicare was beginning to reimburse patients with angina who used EECP therapy. Wow, now that's progress![14]

171

Cold/Flu

RECOMMENDED SUPPLEMENTS

- Vitamin C
- Echinacea/goldenseal
- Beta-glucan
- Zinc lozenges
- Oregano oil
- Olive leaf extract
- N-acetylcysteine (NAC)

We were having a "doctor's night" on the TBN television network several years ago, and I felt like I was coming down with a cold. I was sitting next to Dr. Julian Whitaker on the set, and he gave me his remedy for fighting off a cold. I tried it, and it worked so well I was shocked! This was his remedy: At the first sign of a cold, immediately begin taking 500–1,000 mg. of vitamin C with 8 ounces of water. Take 1,000 mg. every waking hour thereafter for as long as you can tolerate it (without experiencing diarrhea). If you experience diarrhea, reduce your intake of vitamin C and water from every hour to every other hour. Continue until cold symptoms subside.

Also, remember to *think zinc!* Zinc appears to directly block nerve impulses that cause sneezing as well as nasal congestion. A study in the *Annals of Internal Medicine* showed that people who took zinc had shorter colds.[15]

Cold Sores/ Herpes Simplex

 RECOMMENDED SUPPLEMENTS

- Lysine
- Echinacea
- Oregano oil
- Olive leaf extract
- Vitamin B complex (especially B1)

 Burton Goldberg, editor of *Alternative Medicine* magazine, told our audience that anyone who has a chronic problem with this condition should eliminate peanuts and chocolate from their diet because these foods are high in the amino acid arginine, which may trigger outbreaks. He also said recurrent herpes outbreaks often occur after episodes of anxiety and stress, which means that stress reduction can help prevent attacks.[16] Dr. David Wood of Trinity Medical Clinic in Lynwood, Washington suggested that the condition may be related to a high-sugar diet.[17] So check your intake of sugar!

Depression

- St. John's Wort
- L-tyrosine
- EFAs, especially Omega-3
- 5-HTP
- Folic acid
- Vitamin B complex
- SAM-e
- DHEA
- L-phenylalanine
- Natural progesterone

Dr. James Privitera told me that he recommends that women who are depressed have their thyroid checked because depression was often a symptom of low thyroid. Because natural progesterone can help regulate thyroid (which is often affected negatively by estrogen dominance), we agreed that many cases of depression could be helped by natural progesterone. In addition to using the other supplements listed above, I have seen many women make a dramatic recovery from depression simply with the use of natural progesterone. This is especially true in cases where the depression coincides with the menstrual cycle.

Diabetes

RECOMMENDED SUPPLEMENTS
- Magnesium
- Vanadium
- Vitamin C
- Vitamin E
- Vitamin B6
- Chromium
- Coenzyme Q-10
- Vitamin D
- MSM
- Aloe vera
- Alpha lipoic acid
- Inositol

In my years of hosting *Doctor to Doctor,* I have had the great privilege of interviewing so many wonderful physicians regarding the treatment of diabetes. I would like to recommend highly that those of you who would like to approach the treatment of diabetes with natural therapies read the following books:

- *The Diabetes Cure: A Medical Approach That Can Slow, Stop, Even Cure Type 2 Diabetes* by Vern Cherewatenko, M.D. (Cliff Street Books, 1999)
- *The Doctor's Guide to Diabetes and Your Child* by Allan E. Sosin, M.D. (Kensington Pub. Corp., 2000)

These are both wonderful books filled with sound medical knowledge that can help and encourage you as you or a loved one deal with diabetes.

Diabetic Neuropathy

RECOMMENDED SUPPLEMENTS
- Vitamin B complex
- Inositol
- Alpha lipoic acid
- Bilberry

Diabetic neuropathy is a frequent complication of diabetes caused by nerve damage from elevated blood glucose levels. The most common symptoms are numbness, tingling and pain in the feet and legs. To date, clinical trials using alpha lipoic acid (ALA) have been very positive. ALA appears to raise intracellular glutathione levels. A long-term trial called the Nathan I study is being conducted in North America and Europe to clarify these findings.[18]

Recommendations

Eczema/Dry Skin

- EFAs, especially Omega-6
- Zinc
- Milk thistle
- Vitamin E
- Vitamin B complex

Research indicates that many cases of eczema are due to food allergies. Individuals suffering from eczema may improve on a diet that eliminates common allergenic foods. An allergy rotation diet where foods are eliminated and re-added every four days can help pinpoint your allergy.

Patients with eczema appear to have an essential fatty acid deficiency; that is why it is important either to eat more fatty fish (mackerel, herring, salmon) or to supplement the diet with fish oils. Fish oils have significant anti-inflammatory and antiallergy effects. At the same time you should decrease animal fat intake, which can cause inflammation. Zinc ointment has also been found to be beneficial for local pain and itching.

Recommendations

Emphysema, Respiratory Health, Bronchitis

RECOMMENDED SUPPLEMENTS

- Magnesium
- N-acetylcysteine
- Selenium
- Zinc
- Vitamin A
- Echinacea
- Beta-glucan
- Vitamin C

In addition to the supplements listed above, Burton Goldberg, editor of *Alternative Medicine* magazine, told me that lecithin is valuable to help reduce the surface tension of fluids in the lungs, thereby enabling easier fluid elimination.

Recommendations

Eye Health

RECOMMENDED SUPPLEMENTS

- Lutein
- Vitamin C (for cataracts)
- Vitamin E
- MSM
- Taurine (for macular degeneration)
- Gingko biloba
- Bilberry
- N-acetylcysteine
- Alpha lipoic acid (for glaucoma; cataracts)
- Glutathione
- Vitamin A (for macular degeneration)
- Vitamin D (for glaucoma)
- Zinc (for macular degeneration)

Recent research published in the *Archives of Ophthalmology* shows that you can save your sight with vitamins. Researchers found that people at high risk of age-related macular degeneration (AMD) could lower that risk by 25 percent by taking supplements.[19] In AMD, growths in the eyes, called *drusen*, eventually lead to the breakdown of light sensitive cells or to the destruction of the eyes' blood vessels.

Important Note: Adults with blue, green or hazel eyes have a 20 percent increased risk of developing macular degeneration in their lifetime.

If you suffer from dry eyes, eye health researcher Bill Sardi tells us that you need to moisturize the eye from the inside out instead of just using drops. He said people with dry eyes

179

usually have dry hair, dry skin and brittle nails also. To improve the condition you should take fish oils and borage oil (EFAs) along with vitamin B6 and vitamin C. He said you should also try gently squeezing your eyelids with your fingers, which will release some of your natural body oils onto the eye.

Fatigue

RECOMMENDED SUPPLEMENTS

- Zinc
- Coenzyme Q-10
- Vitamin B complex, especially B12
- Vitamin C
- Ginseng
- Olive leaf extract
- Manganese
- DHEA
- Natural progesterone

Dr. Edward Conley, founder and medical director of the Fatigue Clinic of Michigan and author of the book *America Exhausted* (Vitality Press, 1997), told me about the epidemic proportions of fatigued people today. He said the major contributor to the epidemic is stress, which leads to adrenal fatigue. If the adrenal glands become exhausted or depleted, they can no longer produce the hormones that are necessary for energy production.

In addition to the supplements listed above, you may want to investigate a good adrenal support supplement. These are best obtained through a healthcare professional or reputable health food store. They are either derived from a sheep or bovine source—I prefer the sheep source because of the "mad cow" outbreaks that have occurred in some areas of the world.

Fibrocystic Breast Disease

RECOMMENDED SUPPLEMENTS

- Vitamin E
- EFAs, especially Omega-6
- Natural progesterone
- Isoflavones

When I interviewed Dr. John R. Lee, we discussed the predominance of fibrocystic breast disease in women today. He had a simple but powerful message to deliver to women: "Go off birth control pills!" Dr. Lee attributes this near-epidemic situation to the estrogen-dominance syndrome caused by synthetic hormones, and I agree![20] The best thing you can do to restore your breasts to normal consistency is to use natural progesterone. My patients reported wonderful results in an average of three to six months using natural progesterone, and the breast tissue remained normal as long as they continued using it.

Fibromyalgia

RECOMMENDED SUPPLEMENTS

- Vitamins B, B3, B6
- Manganese
- EFAs
- Vitamin E
- Magnesium
- Vitamin C
- Potassium
- SAM-e
- Coenzyme Q-10
- Beta-glucan

Professor Garth L. Nicolson, Institute for Molecular Medicine in Huntington Beach, California, has published over five hundred medical and scientific papers and serves on the editorial boards of fourteen medical and scientific journals. When I interviewed him on *Doctor to Doctor,* he told me that while he was researching Gulf War Syndrome, he discovered that chronic infections underlie many cases of chronic fatigue syndrome.

According to Professor Nicolson, 60 percent of fibromyalgia sufferers have a bacterial or a viral infection from systemic mycoplasmas and many sufferers have both types of infection. These mycoplasmas penetrate the cell and interfere with its structure and ability to produce energy. Antibiotic treatment is used if the chronic infection is indeed found to be the cause of either fibromyalgia or chronic fatigue syndrome.[21]

Recommendations

Fungal Infections

RECOMMENDED SUPPLEMENTS

- Olive leaf extract
- Acidophilus
- Beta-glucan
- Oregano oil
- Aloe vera

Fungal infections can be anything from candidiasis to infected toenails.

Fungi are simple parasitic life forms that can be very difficult to eradicate from the body. Dr. Morton Walker told me that many fungal infections, both within the body and on the skin's surface, including toenails, are effectively treated by the antifungal effects of olive leaf extract.[22] I have seen remarkable results in people who take it, especially people suffering from candida albicans.

Dr. William Kellas recommended this treatment for people with toenail fungus: Apply tea tree oil to the affected areas twice daily. Tea tree oil is available in health food stores. You can also buy acidophilus in soft gel caps, open the capsule and apply the contents directly to the infected toenails twice daily. Remember, though, that fungal infection of the nails is difficult to treat and requires patience. You should start to see a difference gradually in the nail as it improves, growing out thinner and lighter in color.

Gastrointestinal Problems

RECOMMENDED SUPPLEMENTS
- Aloe vera
- Acidophilus
- Licorice root

My favorite remedy for any gastrointestinal problem is aloe vera. I have seen so much anecdotal evidence of the healing powers of aloe when ingested daily. Better yet, a study published in the *Journal of Alternative Medicine* showed that aloe vera juice is effective for treating inflammatory bowel disease.[23] Patients given 2 ounces of aloe vera juice three times daily for seven days reported no incidence of diarrhea after one week. In addition, they had improved bowel regularity and increased energy. Researchers concluded that aloe was able to rebalance the intestines by regulating gastrointestinal pH, improve gastrointestinal motility and reduce populations of certain microorganisms including yeast. Other studies have shown that aloe vera juice helps detoxify the bowel, neutralize stomach acidity and relieve constipation and gastric ulcers.[24]

Another interesting tip comes from Dr. Steven Levine, who brought me a study published in the *New England Journal of Medicine* (considered one of the finest medical journals in the world and usually represents conventional medical opinion). The study said that although the

185

mechanism was not clear, chewing mastic gum could help treat ulcers, gastritis and acid reflux. The dosage used was up to 1 mg. twice daily for two weeks. The gum apparently is effective against *Helicobacter pylori,* which has been found to be strongly associated with duodenal ulcers, gastric ulcers, gastritis and hyperacidity. Mastic gum is a nontoxic herbal gum that can be found in many health food stores.[25]

Hair Health

- Vitamin A
- Vitamin B12
- Biotin
- Folic acid
- Inositol
- Choline
- Vitamin E
- MSM
- PABA

If your hair is excessively dry, you may not be eating enough fat. Diets very low in fat can cause hair to be dry and brittle. Increase your intake of healthful fats from sources like extra-virgin olive oil (Omega-9) and walnuts. You can also take borage oil, an Omega-6 fatty acid, as a supplement. In only a few months, many individuals see their hair return to normal.

When I interviewed Dr. Thierry Hertoghe, an antiaging specialist, at the Seventh Annual Antiaging Conference, he told me that hormones play an important role in hair health. He reported the following:

- If you lose your male hormone, you will lose hair on your head.

- If you lose your female hormone, you will grow hair on your body.

- Hair loss on the head of a female indicates low estrogen.

187

- Diffuse hair loss everywhere indicates low thyroid.

- Hair growth everywhere indicates a hormone imbalance. The use of transdermal estrogen and progesterone is good to remedy such an imbalance.

- Hair growth on a woman's face means her adrenals may be making too much male hormone and not enough cortisol. Adrenal supplements will help restore this balance.[26]

Finally, my good friend and esteemed pharmacologist and antiaging researcher Jim Jamieson told me that he has found that folic acid can help with balding. He said he found that a dose of 5 mg. of folic acid daily will help grow hair.[27] This is equal to about six 800 mcg. capsules daily.

Headaches

RECOMMENDED SUPPLEMENTS

- Magnesium
- Feverfew
- Natural progesterone
- Vitamin B complex
- L-phenylalanine (for migraines)

I have found that natural progesterone is extremely effective in eliminating headaches in women. The changes in estrogen levels that take place in a woman's body during perimenopause, menopause and premenstrually can trigger headaches and/or affect the frequency of headaches. If you consistently have premenstrual headaches, use natural progesterone during the ten days prior to your period each month to restore hormonal balance.

I have had patients tell me that they have suffered for years and then had headaches disappear within three or four months of using natural progesterone. If you are having a migraine headache, apply ¼ to ½ teaspoon of progesterone cream immediately and then every three hours until your symptoms have subsided. You can experiment with the dose to find what works for you. Taking magnesium can also help stop an acute attack.

In my interview with Burton Goldberg, editor of *Alternative Medicine* magazine, he offers this tip that he says can often help stop a migraine headache triggered by an allergic reaction to food or a chemical substance: As soon as the migraine headache begins, dissolve two Alka Seltzer Gold tablets in a glass of water and drink it. This creates an alkaline condition in the body that neutralizes the allergic mechanism. This prevents the migraine from fully developing.[28]

Heart Arrythmias

RECOMMENDED SUPPLEMENTS
- Calcium
- Potassium
- Coenzyme Q-10
- Hawthorn
- Magnesium

Potassium, calcium and magnesium are the best supplements to help control heart arrhythmias. However, if you have multiple episodes, they may be connected to supraventricular arrhythmias or atrial flutters. Heart expert Dr. Kelly Tucker of the Orange County Heart Institute and Research Center has had much success with a procedure called radio-frequency ablation, which involves using radio-frequency energy to destroy the tissue in the heart wall that interferes with the heart's electrical signal and leaves the normal electrical pathways in the heart untouched.[29]

Heart Disease

RECOMMENDED SUPPLEMENTS

- Vitamin E
- Coenzyme Q-10
- Magnesium
- Potassium
- Gingko biloba
- Vitamin B complex
- Folic acid
- EFAs, especially Omega-3
- Vitamin C
- Gugulipid
- Hawthorn
- Carnitine
- Taurine
- Green tea
- Selenium
- Lecithin
- Isoflavones
- DHEA

Over the years I have talked to many experts in the field of heart disease who consider chelation therapy one of the best methods to remove clogging material from the arteries. Chelation therapy is safe when the protocol of the American College of Advancement in Medicine is followed.

EDTA-chelation therapy consists of intravenous drips of an amino acid called ethylene diamine tetraacetic acid. It has been used in the U.S. to relieve hardening of the arteries since 1952.

191

Chelation therapy can help reverse atherosclerosis and is useful for those who have had a heart attack, stroke and transient ischemic attacks.[30]

I also believe in preventative chelation therapy. I have had chelation therapy, and I highly recommend it. On another note, taking one baby aspirin daily (81 mg.) can lower your risk of heart attack.[31]

Herpes

RECOMMENDED SUPPLEMENTS

- Lysine
- EFAs
- Vitamin B complex
- Olive leaf extract
- Echinacea

After the primary infection, the herpes virus becomes a dormant inhabitant within ganglia of the nerves. Recurrences may be stimulated by different factors including stress, food allergies, drugs and certain foods. Chronic, persistent outbreaks are usually seen in people with suppressed immune systems. Therefore the key to the control of herpes infections is a strong immune system. Stress reduction is also an important factor. Many sufferers have decreased their outbreaks by eating foods high in the amino acid lysine such as fish, seafood, chicken, eggs and brewer's yeast in addition to taking supplemental lysine.

193

High Blood Pressure

- Choline
- Vitamin E
- Coenzyme Q-10
- Calcium/magnesium
- EFAs
- Olive leaf extract
- Potassium
- Hawthorn
- Green tea

Garlic and other members of the onion family should be included in the diets of anyone concerned with lowering their blood pressure. Garlic has been shown in some studies to decrease the systolic (bottom number) by 20–30 mmHg and the diastolic (top number) by 10–20 mmHg. Garlic's hypotensive effect is believed to be related to its effect on the autonomic nervous system, the fact that it possesses lipid-lowering qualities and also that it has a high content of sulphur-containing compounds as well as selenium. Selenium is a trace mineral that helps boost the body's ability to guard against platelets sticking together.[32]

High Cholesterol

RECOMMENDED SUPPLEMENTS
- IP6
- Gugulipid
- Green tea
- Copper
- L-carnitine
- Hawthorn
- Lecithin
- Isoflavones
- EFAs

Many specialists have told me that niacin or nicotinic acid (vitamin B3) is one of the most powerful tools available for lowering cholesterol and reducing mortality from fatal heart attacks. Niacin has been found not only to improve the beneficial HDL, but also to lower the dangerous LDL. Doses as low as 1,200 mg. per day have been found to be effective.

Higher doses can give greater results, but these higher doses must be monitored by a physician. I know the statin drugs are being heavily promoted right now on television and in print ads, but there are some serious side effects associated with them. Please ask your doctor about a trial of niacin.

For fruit lovers, here is good news: Fresh berries may slow the buildup of LDL cholesterol (the bad cholesterol that can block arteries). According to research at the University of California at Davis, berries accomplish this with natural substances called phenolic compounds, which act as antioxidants. The berries in order of effectiveness at limiting LDL buildup are blackberries, red raspberries, sweet cherries, blueberries and strawberries.[33]

Immune System

RECOMMENDED SUPPLEMENTS

- Echinacea
- Olive leaf extract
- Aloe vera
- Vitamin C
- Pycnogenol
- Glutamine
- EFAs
- Isoflavones
- IP6
- Zinc
- Folic acid

The thymus gland, which lies just below the thyroid and above the heart, is responsible for many functions of the immune system, including the production of T-cells. As we age, this gland begins to shrink as it is extremely susceptible to free-radical and oxidative damage. Antioxidants can prevent thymic damage and enhance immune function.

In my fascinating interview with Dr. Terry Beardsley, an expert in the field of thymic function, he told me about a thymic fraction called Thymic Protein A that he believes may be one of the most powerful immune regulators ever developed. Dr. Beardsley developed it as a powder that is used sublingually. Watch for this new immune enhancer to become available in health food stores in the future.[34]

Impotence

RECOMMENDED SUPPLEMENTS

- Vitamin E
- Zinc
- EFAs
- Gingko biloba
- Yohimbe
- L-arginine
- Korean ginseng
- Folic acid

Erectile dysfunction can be definitively related to poor health. A majority of all cases are estimated to be due to an organic or physiological (related to the body) condition. Proper diagnosis is vital, because the next step is to correct any underlying organic factor in order to restore sexual function. There are very simple non-invasive tests that can reveal the source of ED. For a more detailed discussion of this condition, you may wish to consult my book *Better Sex for You* (Siloam Press, 2001).

Insomnia

RECOMMENDED SUPPLEMENTS

- Potassium
- Vitamin B complex
- Calcium
- Melatonin
- Valerian
- Kava
- 5-HTP
- St. John's Wort

I did an extensive interview with Dr. Ray Sahelian of the Longevity Research Institute several years ago in which he gave our audience some wonderful advice regarding insomnia. In addition to the supplements listed above, he recommends these important tips in dealing with insomnia:

- Expose yourself to daylight for ten to twenty minutes within one hour of waking up. This exposure stimulates the pituitary gland and "resets" your body clock. (This works, by the way!)

- Also, eating smaller portions of food more frequently, especially protein, can be helpful to sleep. Eat carbohydrates at night, one to three hours prior to bedtime.

- Do physical activity in the late afternoon or early evening as your muscles need to be tired for a good night's sleep.

- The best sleep occurs when the body is cool, so take hot baths one to two hours before bedtime, not immediately before retiring.

- And yes, that glass of milk before bedtime will help (except for those people who are lactose intolerant).[35]

Dr. Edward J. Conley, author of *America Exhausted*, told us that the brain needs at least one hour of darkness to create its own melatonin, so turn off the lights and TV one hour prior to bedtime.[36] On another note, I want to add that women who have problems with insomnia almost always benefit from the use of natural progesterone. It balances the hormones and works as a natural sleep aid. Personally, I rub it on the back of my neck each night before sleep.

Libido Loss

RECOMMENDED SUPPLEMENTS

- Avena sativa
- L-tyrosine
- Natural progesterone
- Tribulus terrestris
- Androstenedione
- Melatonin
- DHEA
- Ginseng
- NADH

I recently researched the loss of libido when I wrote my book *Better Sex for You,* as I have mentioned. If you would like to research this topic in-depth, it is full of great information that will help you with this very real problem—it is NOT all in your head! From that research I concluded that libido loss affects about one in three married couples, either the man, the woman or sometimes both at the same time. Though the problem is real, the good news is: Supplements work!

My favorite treatment is ¼ teaspoon of natural progesterone twice daily. Many women tell me that they have their libido restored within three to four months of using natural progesterone and feel like young brides again. I highly recommend that you give this a try along with some of the other supplements listed.

Liver Problems

- Milk thistle
- Alpha lipoic acid
- Glutathione
- Inositol
- Choline

Dr. Sandra Cabot, author of *The Healthy Liver & Bowel* (Celestial Arts, 2000) and *The Liver Cleansing Diet* (Ten Speed Press, 1998), gives the following vital principles for a healthy liver:

Eat some raw vegetables or fruit at every meal. Avoid all trans-fatty acids, artificial sweeteners and foods that you know have been treated with pesticides. (I suggest you pick the two or three fruits or vegetables you eat the most and buy the organic kind.) Drink lots of water to flush out toxins (eight to ten glasses daily). Avoid overeating as this overworks the liver. Eat foods that are known to help liver function, like legumes, kiwi, garlic, essential fatty acids and flax.

It is important to recognize these symptoms of impaired liver health: history of mysterious illness, headaches, tired all the time, feeling overheated, elevated cholesterol levels (often the last symptom) and cellulite (toxin buildup in the fat cells). Remember, our liver pumps toxins and poisons out of the body; hence it is very important to keep our livers healthy!

Recommendations

Menopause

RECOMMENDED SUPPLEMENTS

- Natural progesterone
- Isoflavones
- Dong quai
- Black cohosh
- Vitamin B complex
- Calcium/magnesium
- Vitamin E
- Red clover
- Pregnenolone
- Panax ginseng
- EFAs

I think the single most perpetrated myth about menopause is that estrogen deficiency is the primary cause of symptoms. A second related myth is that estrogen levels fall to zero after menopause. These assumptions are untrue. Estrogen levels will drop and/or fluctuate, but you will always make some estrogen because it is made in your fat cells.

Instead, it is progesterone levels that fall to zero during menopause. In an effort to stay balanced, your body in essence "turns down" its estrogen receptors. If you add natural progesterone and, if you have no history of breast cancer, some phyto-estrogen, you can stabilize most of your symptoms. If you continue to have hot flashes on natural hormones, do not resort to going onto synthetic hormones. (No synthetics, PLEASE—you will increase your risk of breast cancer by

203

60–85 percent.) There are several things you can do. Vitamin E especially can help eliminate hot flashes. See my website www.askdrhelen.com for many other tips.

Another myth many physicians tell their female patients is that synthetic hormone treatment (HRT) helps prevent heart attacks. It has now been proven that this is simply not so. The American Heart Association is now advising post-menopausal women with heart disease not to resort to HRT and is telling those without heart disease not to count on HRT to protect them against it. In fact, recent clinical trials released halfway through an eight-year study showed that the HRT group of women had more heart attacks, strokes and blood clots than women taking a placebo. In fact, the surprising conclusion was reached that HRT actually increased a woman's risk. The final results are not expected until 2005, but this research has cast great doubt on any benefit for the heart from synthetic hor-mones.[37] Instead, a woman must protect her heart just as men do: healthy diet, lifestyle changes and good nutrition and supplementation (COQ-10, folic acid and so on).

Note: If you are currently taking synthetic hor-mones and would like to stop depending on them, please visit my website at www.askdrhelen.com. I have weaning instructions posted for you.

Menstrual Cramps

RECOMMENDED SUPPLEMENTS

- Natural progesterone
- Black cohosh
- Magnesium
- Vitamin B complex
- Valerian root
- Feverfew
- St. John's Wort
- Dong quai

Cramping can be attributed to a condition called estrogen dominance and can sometimes be a symptom of many diseases, including endometriosis. One of the best tips I can give you for menstrual cramping is to use natural progesterone, which balances the effects of too much estrogen. Use ¼ tsp. daily from days 12–26 of your cycle. You can rub the cream right onto the abdomen during severe episodes and experience much relief. It may take up to six months of use, but in the majority of my cases, women report significant relief of menstrual cramps; some women report complete cessation of cramping.

205

Mental Function/ Memory

RECOMMENDED SUPPLEMENTS

- L-glutamine
- Gingko biloba
- Vitamin B complex
- Phosphatidylserine
- Pregnenolone
- DMAE
- Acetyl L-carnitine
- Vitamin E
- Lecithin
- DHEA

Did you ever wonder what is actually happening to your brain that causes mental function to decline? According to Dr. Julian Whitaker of the Whitaker Wellness Institute, the following things occur: Your brain size begins to shrink. As early as age thirty, the connections between brain cells (neurons) start to disappear and the brain literally shrinks in size. Your neurotransmitters (chemical messengers) decline. One that is most affected is acetylcholine, which is the neuro-transmitter involved in learning and storing new information. Also, production of pregnenolone, the hormone that helps combat mental fatigue and boost energy, begins to drop. Finally, circulation becomes less efficient as we age, so less oxygen and glucose (fuel) are delivered to the brain.[38]

The good news is that each of these natural occurrences can be helped with brain-boosting nutrients and supplements. Another interesting fact discovered through research at the University of California, San Francisco, is that six thousand older women, average age seventy, who walked daily decreased their chances of losing their memory and retained more mental clarity. For every mile the women walked, they dropped their chances of mental problems by 13 percent.[39]

Does walking sound boring? Then perhaps you could consider taking up golf and walking the eighteen holes!

Miscarriage

- Natural progesterone
- Vitamin E
- Bioflavonoids

 According to Dr. John R. Lee, women with a history of miscarriage may have what is called luteal phase failure. This condition exists when the follicles ovulate normally but fail to continue their progesterone production at levels necessary for successful implantation of the fertilized egg and development of the embryo. Luteal phase failure can be prevented by using natural progesterone. These women need to increase and maintain their progesterone levels.

Dr. Lee advises that as soon as pregnancy is confirmed by a blood test, a woman at risk for miscarriage should start using progesterone cream. Women who are already using progesterone cream should simply continue, but increase the dose. In the first month, use ¼ tsp. twice daily. After the first month, the dose can be increased gradually to ½ tsp. twice daily. After the third month of pregnancy, the progesterone production in the placenta increases enough that the supplemental progesterone may not be necessary. However, it is safe to continue the cream throughout the pregnancy, stopping about one week before the expected delivery date.[40]

Dr. Perry Ratcliff also told me that women who have periodontal disease also have a higher risk of miscarriage.[41] So, please, exercise proper dental hygiene if you are trying to get pregnant!

Osteoporosis

RECOMMENDED SUPPLEMENTS
- Natural progesterone
- Vitamin D
- Calcium
- Magnesium
- Boron
- Vitamin A
- Lysine
- Manganese

Many physicians erroneously tell their patients that estrogen will grow bone. Ladies, the fact is that synthetic estrogen does not help you to build new bone. It simply keeps the old bone in place. Studies show that after about five to seven years, the stabilizing effects of the synthetic hormones wear off and the old bone becomes very vulnerable. It is progesterone that helps build new bone, natural progesterone, not synthetic progestin.[42]

Studies by Dr. John R. Lee showed that women built up to 37 percent new bone using natural progesterone. That's wonderful news, but even better news is that the worst cases had the best results.[43] If you have been told you have osteoporosis or if you are at risk, PLEASE get some natural progesterone and use it liberally.

Periodontal Disease

RECOMMENDED SUPPLEMENTS
- Coenzyme Q-10
- Folic acid
- Aloe vera
- Vitamin C

Please do not be careless about the signs of periodontal disease: bleeding gums and receding gum line. Periodontal disease has been related to heart problems and also to miscarriage, as we mentioned. Dr James Privitera told me that receding gums usually correlate with bone loss, which means a great risk for osteoporosis.[44] If you notice receding gums, he suggests you have a mineral test to check your calcium levels.

PMS

RECOMMENDED SUPPLEMENTS

- Natural progesterone
- Vitamin B6 (time release form)
- Vitamin B complex
- Gamma linoleic acid (GLA)
- Calcium/magnesium
- EFAs
- Vitamin E
- Black cohosh
- Dong quai
- Licorice root

Common PMS symptoms are anxiety, bloating, breast tenderness, cramping, crying spells, depression, headaches, insomnia, low back pain, mood swings, sugar cravings, acne and weight gain. Both Dr. John R. Lee and I agree that generally women with PMS symptoms have elevated estrogen levels or high estrogen levels in relation to their progesterone levels.

Stress, environmental toxins (known as xenoestrogens), foods containing estrogenic substances and birth control pills can all cause this condition known as estrogen dominance. The use of natural progesterone from days 12–26 of the menstrual cycle can markedly ease and even completely eliminate the symptoms of PMS.

Magnesium is also very important for the formation of mood-regulating neurotransmitters. When you consider that chocolate is high in magnesium, it makes sense that women crave it

211

while suffering from PMS. Other foods that are good sources of magnesium are kale, nuts, figs and pumpkinseeds.

Prostate

RECOMMENDED SUPPLEMENTS

- Saw palmetto
- Zinc
- Pygeum
- Selenium
- Natural progesterone
- Vitamin E

A study in the July 2001 issue of *Urology* showed that flaxseed can slow the progression of prostate cancer. Researchers at Duke University found that flaxseed contains a fiber compound called lignan that can help slow tumor growth by binding to the male hormone testosterone, which can to contribute to the progression of prostate cancer.[45] Flaxseed also contains Omega-3 fatty acids, which have been shown to slow cancer growth in animal studies. According to a recent study, lycopene, found in tomato products, has also been found to lower prostate cancer risks.[46]

Over the years, many antiaging experts have told me that natural progesterone was helpful in treating an enlarged prostate, but it was Dr. Lee who told me that the prostate is made from the same embryonic tissue as the uterus. So, just as natural progesterone helps protect against the negative effects of environmental estrogens on the uterus, it does the same thing for the prostate. Remember, progesterone is neither a specific male or female hormone, so men can use it as well as women. I recommend ¼ tsp. twice daily. Also, if you are over fifty-five years of age, it is very effective in enhancing libido.

Psoriasis

RECOMMENDED SUPPLEMENTS
- EFAs
- Folic acid
- MSM
- Vitamin B complex
- Milk thistle
- Aloe vera
- Zinc

Strictly speaking, psoriasis is not an outward skin disorder; it is a condition caused by a metabolic disturbance that causes the skin cells to divide at a highly increased rate. It is simply too fast for the cells to be shed, so they accumulate and result in patches of skin that may be thickened, reddened and covered with silvery scales. Experts believe that anxiety or stress triggers psoriasis attacks, as well as essential fatty acid deficiencies and low digestive enzymes, specifically hydrochloric acid and folic acid deficiency.[47]

Experts also recommend avoiding all alcohol as this is known to worsen psoriasis to a considerable degree. Also, curtail the consumption of animal fats as well since this too will trigger the inflammatory response.

Essential fatty acids are extremely important in the treatment of psoriasis as they inhibit the production of inflammatory compounds. In addition to supplementing with EFAs, also try to consume seafood high in Omega-3 fatty acids such as salmon, sardines and mackerel.

Rheumatoid Arthritis

RECOMMENDED SUPPLEMENTS

- Beta carotene
- L-cysteine
- Vitamin C
- Vitamin B12
- EFAs
- Pregnenolone
- Glucosamine

If you suffer from rheumatoid arthritis, it is important for you to know that approximately one-third of all those who struggle with this condition are sensitive to solanine, a substance that is found in the nightshade plants. These include peppers, eggplant, tomatoes, potatoes and tobacco. Eliminating these from your diet can greatly reduce the signs and symptoms of rheumatoid arthritis.[48]

Sexual Energy

RECOMMENDED SUPPLEMENTS

- Gingko biloba
- L-arginine
- Folic acid
- Korean ginseng
- Tribulus terrestris
- Zinc
- Natural progesterone
- DHEA

Loss of libido is the number one question I answer for my viewers when I reply to their mail. That is why I finally wrote the book *Better Sex for You.* I really believe it should be subtitled *There Is Hope for Your Sex Life,* as so many of the people I talk to sound hopeless. There is much that can be done for you to restore you to your natural sexual vitality. The supplements listed above will help you, with natural progesterone being my first recommendation for women. There are many more answers for you in the book, or you may write to me or visit my website at www.askdrhelen.com.

Skin Problems

RECOMMENDED SUPPLEMENTS

- EFAs, especially Omega-6
- Vitamin A
- Oregano oil
- Vitamin B6
- Folic acid
- Milk thistle
- Vitamin D
- Zinc

In addition to the above recommendations, I strongly suggest that you exfoliate your skin at least twice a week, even if you have dry skin. It is a fallacy that women with dry skin cannot exfoliate. You need to remove those dead skin cells to get to the fresh, glowing skin below. I also advocate the use of alpha hydroxy acids, vitamin A and vitamin C serum to treat problem skin or rejuvenate aging skin. For more answers to your skin problems, please visit my website at www.heavenlyskin.com.

Sperm Deficiency

(Low Sperm Count)

 RECOMMENDED SUPPLEMENTS

- Selenium
- Zinc
- L-arginine
- Tribulus terrestris
- Vitamin A

 If a low sperm count is your problem, please take heart. Modern medicine has provided a host of ways to aid you. Cappy Rothman, who practices in Los Angeles, California, and is one of the foremost male infertility experts in the United States, has developed a program by which even one sperm can be used to successfully facilitate pregnancy![49]

Stress/Adrenal Health

RECOMMENDED SUPPLEMENTS

- Tyrosine
- Magnesium
- Vitamin C
- Vitamin B complex
- Natural progesterone
- Pregnenolone
- Melatonin
- Ginseng
- Licorice root
- DHEA
- Kava

Dr. Vincent Giampapa, founding member of the American Board of Antiaging Medicine and president of the Longevity Institute International told me on the set of *Doctor to Doctor* that stress can be defined as "the feeling of being constantly in a hurry." This keeps cortisol levels high and damages brain cells, which leads to memory loss and aging of the brain, thus making it difficult for the body to function properly. His advice: "Slow down. Make a conscious effort to move more slowly, but efficiently."[50] I think we would all do well to heed this advice.

My mentor, Dr. John R. Lee, taught me many years ago that progesterone helps balance cortisol levels. It can also help restore energy and correct hormonal imbalance. Chronic stress

Recommendations

leads to chronic high cortisol levels in the body, which means the body is in a state of constant hormonal imbalance.[51]

Tinnitus
(Ringing in Ears)

RECOMMENDED SUPPLEMENTS
- Gingko biloba
- Magnesium
- Echinacea
- Coenzyme Q-10
- Choline
- Zinc
- Vitamin B12

Dr. David Wood of Trinity Medical Clinic, Lynnwood, Washington, told me that tinnitus can be caused by a dysfunction of the auditory nerve. Although no actual studies have been done on tinnitus patients, Dr. Wood said that phosphatidylserine is believed to help repair nerve cell membrane damage. He recommended that tinnitus sufferers may want to give this a trial.[52] In another study, 47 percent of people with tinnitus were found to be deficient in vitamin B12.[53]

Urinary Tract Infections

RECOMMENDED SUPPLEMENTS

- Pygeum
- Acidophilus
- Echinacea

Menopausal women are often prone to frequent urinary tract infections because hormonal deficiency causes thinning of the urogenital system. Because estrogen receptors are found in the bladder and the lower urinary tract, a good natural progesterone/estrogen cream can help keep the tissue in this area healthy and infection-resistant. If the infection is bacterial, sometimes treatment must involve a course of antibiotics.

One of the best remedies I have ever found for temporary relief of a urinary tract infection is parsley tea. To prepare, take two bunches of regular parsley. Boil in three to four inches of water for twenty minutes. Let cool, then drink the tea. It is very soothing to the bladder!

Viral Infections

- Olive leaf extract
- Vitamin C
- Zinc
- Quercetin (bioflavonoids)
- Echinacea

Many experts have told me that the best defense against a viral disease is to take as much vitamin C as you can tolerate (excessive amounts cause diarrhea). Once you have reached the point of bowel intolerance (diarrhea), cut back slightly until a maintenance dose is reached. In many conditions, symptoms are greatly reduced, especially in dealing with common cold viruses.

Weight Loss/ Appetite Suppressants

RECOMMENDED SUPPLEMENTS

- 5-HTP
- Chromium
- Vanadium
- Green tea
- Coenzyme Q-10
- L-phenylalanine
- DHEA
- L-tyrosine
- L-glutamine

Two tips that might help you in your battle with weight control:

1. Researchers looking into the metabolic effects of green tea have found that it may be able to help you shed pounds. A Swiss study found that green tea extract increased the level of the body's fat-burning fires and kept them stoked (*American Journal of Clinical Nutrition*).[54] The results led the researchers to conclude that green tea may help boost fat thermogenesis, the incineration of fat by the body's microscopic metabolic fat furnaces.

2. Dr. Vincent Giampapa, founding member of the American Board of Antiaging Medicine and president of the Longevity Institute International, told me that anyone trying to lose weight should munch on raw

spinach because spinach contains 43 percent protein! You will be eating almost no calories and will be getting your protein at the same time. No more complaining of feeling weak while dieting![55]

Wrinkles

RECOMMENDED SUPPLEMENTS

- EFAs
- Vitamin E
- Pycnogenol
- MSM

Dr. Julian Whitaker and pharmacologist Jim Jamieson gave me the best advice on treating wrinkles. It absolutely works, and I have been recommending it for years—topical vitamin C! Extensive studies at Duke University Medical Center and at the University of California, San Diego demonstrated that serums containing highly concentrated doses of vitamin C can effectively stimulate collagen and elastin tissues in the dermis layer of the skin. With the formation of new collagen, skin tone was restored, the skin appeared smoother and plumper, and the appearance of wrinkles and sagging was visibly reduced.[56]

Note: In order to achieve these antiaging results the vitamin C must be in a specially formulated and stabilized state. Do not rub vitamin C from a pill or capsule directly onto the skin as it will not be effective. Oral vitamin C is also ineffective. My research into vitamin C serums has shown me that vitamin C-ester is the key ingredient to look for in your C serum. For more information on antiaging skin care, you may wish to visit my website, www.heavenlyskin.com.

Three Winning Ws
Word, Water and Walk

Dear Readers,

Remember, you were created in a garden—not in a laboratory!

In addition to eating a healthy diet balanced with necessary supplements, there are three more ingredients I would like you to remember that are vital for your health. To remind yourself of these important elements of health, you can just think of the three winning Ws: Word, water and walk.

Word

The first winning W involves your daily reading and confessing the Word of God, receiving His promises for healing and health. Meditation on God's Word is essential to your mental and spiritual health, which directly affects your physical health. I encourage you to spend at least a few minutes every day quietly meditating on God's love for you as He reveals that love through His Word.

Water

You should drink at least one-half of your body weight in ounces of water each day. For most of us, this is about eight to ten glasses of water daily.

Your body requires adequate water to function properly. Your neurological pathways require water to function normally. As you dehydrate, your brain will actually shrink. Also, if you lack energy, it is very possible that you are dehydrated. Water helps deliver

227

oxygen throughout the body's tissues that is necessary for energy. If you have an illness or disease, water helps detoxify your cells and flush disease-causing toxins out of the body.

Water also helps nutrients circulate throughout the body, improves kidney function and prevents kidney stones. Other vital functions water facilitates in the body include:

- Lubricating our joints
- Preventing constipation
- Keeping skin moist and supple
- Helping keep respiratory tract healthy

I recommend filtered or bottled water, especially if your water is highly chlorinated or contains unsafe levels of fluoride or chemicals.

Walk

I know many of you may not like to do strenuous exercise; some of you may not be physically able to do it. But most of us can walk! Inactivity is a major cause of our physical as well as mental ills. A total lack of physical activity can cause our brains and bodies to deteriorate. Walking works the major lower body muscles and is considered one of the most valuable of all exercise forms.

Start walking. Begin by walking to the end of your block or street or even just to the mailbox. You don't have to change drastically overnight—just begin including a short walk in your day. Perhaps you can find a buddy and walk and pray together. Start with just five minutes and see if you can work up to a half-hour of steady walking.

You can do it—one step at a time. I did! Look at the benefits you will derive from your walking:

> **BENEFITS FROM WALKING**
> ■ Increases oxygen flow to the brain
> ■ Will keep brain young and vital
> ■ Will create a feeling of well-being
> ■ Increases energy levels
> ■ Relieves stress, diminishing cortisol levels
> ■ Combats depression
> ■ Increases sexual energy and performance
> ■ Strengthens cardiovascular system
> ■ Improves circulation
> ■ Burns calories
> ■ Keeps joints limber
> ■ Boosts immune system
> ■ Improves sleep patterns
> ■ Helps lower blood pressure

I am convinced that you will enjoy a much better quality of life by simply adding the three winning Ws to your daily routine. It has made a wonderful difference for me!

Cordially,
Helen Pensanti, M.D.

Resource Guide

HORMONE CREMES

My private formulas of the natural progesterone creme and the red clover phyto-estrogen creme can both be found in Sav-On, Osco, Jewel and selected Albertson's stores across the country. They may also be found in many other local health food stores.

They are sold under the names *Pro-HELP* (containing USP progesterone) and *Menopause Relief Cream* (a progesterone-phyto-estrogen blend).

WOMEN'S HORMONE QUESTIONS

If you have any specific questions related to women's hormone balance, please visit my website for updated studies and information: www.askdrhelen.com.

I also highly recommend that you obtain one or all of Dr. John R. Lee's books:

- *What Your Doctor May Not Tell You About Menopause.* New York: Warner Books, 1996.
- *What Your Doctor May Not Tell You About Premenopause.* New York: Warner Books, 1999.
- *What Your Doctor May Not Tell You About Breast Cancer.* New York: Warner Books, 2002.

These books are an excellent resource for your questions about how hormone balance can affect a woman's health.

LIBIDO, SEXUAL ENERGY AND NATURAL HORMONE QUESTIONS

My book *Better Sex for You* (Siloam Press, 2001) is available at Amazon.com, Christian bookstores and through my website at www.askdrhelen.com.

The C-serum wrinkle treatment can be ordered at www.heavenlyskin.com.

For an excellent source of quality vitamins, minerals and supplements, I recommend Judy Lindberg McFarland's company:

Nutrition Express
P. O. Box 3699
Torrance, CA 90510
(800) 338-7979

To receive the following free pamphlets and other helpful literature:

1. Natural Hormones Made Easy

2. Top 10 Reasons to Get Off Synthetic Hormones

3. Latest Hormone Studies/Guidelines

WRITE TO:

Helen Pensanti, M.D.
P. O. Box 7530
Newport Beach, CA 92658
www.askdrhelen.com
(877) 880-0170
E-mail: info@askdrhelen.com

Notes

Please note: The author does not intend to recommend all information found on the websites listed; they serve only as references for the comments regarding specific conditions she has discussed.

BEFORE YOU READ ON

1. *Webster's New World Dictionary of American English,* Third College Edition (New York: Simon and Schuster, 1988), s.v. "vitamin."
2. Ibid., s.v. "mineral."
3. Ibid., s.v. "amino acid."
4. Ibid., s.v. "supplement."

VITAMINS

1. *Taber's Cyclopedic Medical Dictionary,* 18th edition (Philadelphia: F. A. Davis Company, 1997), s.v. "antioxidant."
2. *Prevention's Healing With Vitamins,* Alice Feinstein, ed. (Emmaus, PA: Rodale Press, 1998), 477.

OTHER NATURAL SUPPLEMENTS

1. F. Jordan, "An Immuno-Potentiating Super Hero-Beta-1,3/1,6-glucan Derived from Yeast Cell Wall," *Macrophage Technologies Publication* (1998): 1–4.
2. Schultz et al., "Association of Macrophage Activation with Anti-tumor Activity by Synthetic and Biologic Agents," *Cancer Res.* 37 (1997): 3338–3343.
3. Rovati et al., *International Journal of Tissue Reactions* 14 (1992): 243–245.
4. E. S. Johnson, N. P. Kadam, D. M. Hylands et al., "Efficacy of feverfew as a prophylactic treatment of migraine," *British Medical Journal* 291 (1985): 569–573.
5. L. Stephen Coles, M.D., Ph.D., *The IP6 with Inositol*

Question and Answer Book (Topanga, CA: Freedom Press, 1999).

6. Ibid.

7. *Taber's Cyclopedic Medical Dictionary,* s.v. "estradiol."

8. Megan Garvey, "FDA Warns That Kava Use May Cause Liver Damage," *Los Angeles Times* (March 26, 2002): A14.

9. Source obtained from the Internet: Meg McGowan, "Herbs to Prevent Cancer," *Conscious Choice* (February 2001): www.consciouschoice.com/herbs/herbs1402.html. Accessed June 18, 2002.

10. *Taber's Cyclopedic Medical Dictionary,* s.v. "aldosterone."

11. Associated Press, "Herb Seems to Interfere With Chemo," *Los Angeles Times* (April 9, 2002): A14.

RECOMMENDATIONS FOR COMMON CONDITIONS

1. James E. Fulton, M.D., Ph.D., *Acne Rx* (Self-published, 2001), 172–174.

2. *Lancet* 356 (2000): 1573–1574.

3. M. Sano et al., "A controlled trial of selegihine, alpha-tocopherol, or both as a treatment for Alzheimer's disease," *New England Journal of Medicine* 336 (April 24, 1997): 1216–1222. Also, Julian Whitaker, M.D., "Antioxidants and Memory Function," obtained from the Internet at www.drwhitaker.com. Accessed July 2, 2002.

4. Bill Sardi, *The Iron Time Bomb* (Self-published, 1999), 145–154. Also, source obtained from the Internet: Bill Sardi, "Media Overlooks Human Studies on Vitamin C," *Nutrition Science News* (August 2001): Transcript available at www.newhope.com/ffn/ffn_backs/ guide_2001/media.cfm.

5. Sardi, *The Iron Time Bomb.* Available on Internet at www.askbillsardi.com.

6. Dr. Ray Sahelian was interviewed on *Doctor to Doctor* on the topic of brain health and fitness. The show

aired on August 29, 2000. Also found on the Internet: www.raysahelian.com.

7. Source obtained from the Internet: NutriNotes, vol. 4, no. 6 (November–December 1997): Transcript available at www.nutrinotes.com/novdec97-simple.htm.

8. Joseph Pizzorno and Michael Murray, *Encyclopedia of Natural Medicine* (Rocklin, CA: Prima Publishing, 1991), 148–155.

9. Dr. Stephen Levine was interviewed on *Doctor to Doctor* on the topic of asthma on February 20, 2001.

10. C. Chen, N. Weiss, P. Newcomb, W. Bartow and E. White, "Hormone Replacement Therapy in Relation to Breast Cancer," *JAMA* 287 (February 13, 2002).

11. P. E. Mohr, D.Y. Wang, W. M. Gregory, M. A. Richards and I. S. Fentiman, "Serum Progesterone and Prognosis in Operable Breast Cancer," *British Journal of Cancer* 73 (1996): 1552–1555.

12. Source obtained from the Internet: www.atkinscenter.com.

13. Francisco Contreras, *The Hope of Living Cancer Free* (Lake Mary, FL: Siloam Press, 2000). Also see the Internet: www.cancure.org/oasis_hospital.htm.

14. Source obtained from the Internet: Treatment Benefit in the EECP; www.mercola.com/2001/jul/14/heart_therapy.htm.

15. *Annals of Internal Medicine* 133 (2000): 245.

16. R. J. Derman, "Counseling the Herpes Genitalis Patient," *Journal of Reproductive Medicine* 31, suppl. 5 (May 1986): 439–444.

17. Dr. David Wood was interviewed on *Doctor to Doctor,* which aired on May 9, 2000.

18. L. Packer, E. H. Witt and H. J. Tritschler, *Lipoic Acid as a Biological Antioxidant, Free Radical Biology and Medicine* 19.2 (1995): 227–250.

19. Source obtained from the Internet: "AREDS: Nutrition Can Slow or Prevent Vision Loss from AMD," www.allaboutvision.com/conditions/amd_news.htm.

20. John R. Lee, M.D., *What Your Doctor May Not Tell You*

About Menopause (New York: Warner Books, Inc., 1996).

21. Garth L. Nicolson, M. Nasralla, J. Haier and N. Nicolson, "Treatment of Systemic Mycoplasmal Infections in Gulf War Illness, Chronic Fatigue and Fibromyalgia Syndromes," *Intern. J. Medicine* (1998): 123–128.

22. Dr. Morton Walker, *Olive Leaf Extract* (New York: Kensington Publishing Corp., 1997), 155–159.

23. "13 Ways Aloe Can Help," *Alternative Medicine* (March 1999): 56–60.

24. Ibid.

25. "Letters to the Editor, *New England Journal of Medicine* (December 1998).

26. Source obtained from the Internet: "GHR15youngernow," www.ghr15youngernow.com.

27. Jim Jamieson was interviewed on *Doctor to Doctor* on the topic of antiaging, which aired September 6, 1999.

28. *Alternative Medicine: The Definitive Guide,* compiled the Burton Goldberg Group (Tiburon, CA: Future Medicine Publishing, Inc., 1993, 1999), 696.

29. Kelly J. Tucker, M.D. was interviewed on *Doctor to Doctor,* which aired on September 7, 1998. See also Internet source: "New Heart Technologies Will Save Thousands More…," www.medtech1.com/success/device_stories.cfm/22/1.

30. *Alternative Medicine: The Definitive Guide,* 126–129.

31. Harris Gelberg, M.D., "'Final Report' on the Aspirin Component of the Physician's Health Study," *Highlights* 11 (Spring 1988).

32. *Lancet* II (1969): 962, 800; *Journal of Traditional Chinese Medicine* 6 (1986): 117.

33. *Journal Agriculture and Food Chemistry* (September 12, 1998), Web edition. See also source obtained from the Internet: "Healthy Bites," www.phillyburbs.com/food/features/0501healthybites.htm.

34. D. J. Fletcher, "Thymic Protein A," *Alternative Medicine* (July 2000): 28–32.

35. Source found on the Internet: www.raysahelian.com.
36. Dr. Edward J. Conley, *America Exhausted* (n.p.: Vitality Press, 1998).
37. *Julian Whitaker's Health & Healing,* Vol. 12, No. 2 (February 2002): 1–2.
38. *Archives Internal Medicine* 161 (2001): 1703–1708.
39. Rita Rubin, "Research Casts Doubt on HRT's Heart Benefits," *USA Today* (July 24, 2001); Rosie Mestel, "Hormone Therapy May Not Benefit the Heart," *Los Angeles Times* (July 24, 2001); individual studies in *JAMA* 226: 652–657 and *JAMA* 280: 605–613.
40. Source obtained from the Internet: "Progesterone Used to Treat Osteoporosis, Miscarriage," *The John R. Lee, M.D. Medical Newsletter* (September 1998): 3; www.johnleemd.com/books.html.
41. Source obtained from the Internet: www.exceptional-practice.com/gp_ow.htm.
42. Source obtained from the Internet: "Discontinuing Hormone Replacement Therapy Does Not Accelerate Bone Loss," March 25, 2002, www.medem.com. Accessed June 18, 2002.
43. John R. Lee, M.D., *Natural Progesterone: The Multiple Roles of a Remarkable Hormone* (Sebastopol, CA: BLL Publishing, 1993), 76–88.
44. *New York State Journal of Medicine* (February 1975): 335.
45. "Flaxseed & Prostate," *Julian Whitaker's Health & Healing,* vol. 12, no. 2 (February 2002): 5; source also obtained from the Internet: www.dukenews.duke.edu/med/flaxseed.htm.
46. "Tomatoes and Lycopene in Prostate Cancer Risks," *Julian Whitaker's Health & Healing,* vol. 11, no. 1 (January 2001): 5.
47. *Alternative Medicine: The Definitive Guide,* 965.
48. Carlton Fredericks, *Arthritis: Don't Learn to Live With It* (n.p.: The Berkeley Publishing Group, 1981).
49. Source obtained from the Internet: Center for Male Reproduction, www.malereproduction.com.

50. Robert Goldman, M.D., D.O., Ph.D., *Brain Fitness* (New York: Doubleday, 1999), 82. Source also obtained from the Internet: www.giampapainstitute.com/gia-about_giampapa.

51. Lee, *What Your Doctor May Not Tell You About Menopause,* 342.

52. Dr. David Wood was interviewed on *Doctor to Doctor* on the topic of tinnitus, which aired on May 22, 2000.

53. *Alternative Medicine* (January 2002): 19.

54. *Am Jrnl Cl. Nut.* 70 (December 1999): 1040–1045.

55. Dr. Vincent Giampapa, "Anti-Aging Research and Advice," Seventh Annual Anti-Aging Conference, aired on *Doctor to Doctor* August 9, 1999.

56. N. V. Perricone, "Topical Vitamin C Ester (Ascorbyl Palmitate)," adapted from The First Annual Symposium on Aging Skin, San Diego, *California Journal of Dermatology* 5 (1997): 162–170.